Wi$e Up, Women!

A GUIDE TO FISCAL AND PHYSICAL WELL-BEING

Jeannette Bajalia

Woman's Worth® LLC
JACKSONVILLE, FLORIDA

Jeannette Bajalia/Woman's Worth®
4655 Salisbury Road, Suite 100
Jacksonville, FL 32256
www.womans-worth.com

Book layout ©2013 BookDesignTemplates.com

Wi$e Up, Women!/ Jeannette Bajalia. — 3rd ed.
ISBN 978-1547293247

Contents

To my mother, who lived a life full of purpose and passion, demonstrating unconditional love and service to her family and friends. She approached many life challenges — from the loss of her newborn babies to the unexpected loss of the love of her life — with unwavering faith, courage, conviction, and determination. Her godly wisdom and strength in turning tragedy into triumph is the legacy she leaves to her family and the lives she touched navigating her elder years with grace and dignity until the day the Lord called her to His side.

My heartfelt thanks go to all the wise women in my life: my mother, sisters, mentors, colleagues, and friends who were instrumental in helping me grow in wisdom and character personally and professionally. May this book touch your life and create a future with deeper purpose and passion for the seeds God planted in your lives.

"For God did not give us a spirit of timidity (a spirit of cowardice, of craven and cringing and fawning fear), but [He has given us a spirit] of power and of love and of calm and well-balanced mind and discipline and self-control."

—2 TIMOTHY 1:7

Foreword

Welcome to the third edition of "Wi$e Up, Women: A Guide to Total Fiscal and Physical Well-Being." The old adage, "the third time is a charm" might apply, but you'll have to read it to find out.

Why a third edition? I released the first edition in 2012. When I was doing the initial research in 2011 and 2012, trying to find sound data on women and finances or women and health care was quite challenging, and I certainly didn't find much information pertaining to the unique needs facing women who are planning for retirement. Even more alarming was the fact that I didn't find much research data on finance-induced stress with women, and how lifestyle impacts women's longevity. You might say that my first edition was ahead of its time. Yet, all my trouble (both the trouble that I've gone to and the trouble that I've caused) is paying off; the industry is changing, and people are taking notice of women's unique struggles. Here we are today in 2017, and there is more compelling data pertaining to women and money, longevity, and health care costs. The industry is finally starting to track women-specific data. This third edition updates the original data and has even more nuanced information about strategies for coping with specific challenges. However, the core message of my original version remains fundamentally unchanged: all women, young and old, need to get our heads out of the sand and get more intimately involved in planning for a long, active, and healthy life.

As I was reading this new version as a 65-year-old woman (Oh yes, since the first printing of this book, I became a proud Medicare-card-carrying senior!), I realized that I have done many women a disservice. Why, you ask? Because I haven't promoted the message of this book and shouted it from the mountain tops from the East Coast to the West Coast and everywhere in between. After reading the newly edited version, I said to myself, "WOW, that's a really good read and ever-so-helpful in planning for a financially sound future." I realized my mistake in not recognizing the nuggets of gold buried in the pages of "Wi$e Up, Women!" Most importantly, the first time I published this book, I hadn't realized how simple it is to protect your financial future—simple, yet not easy without the help of resources such as this book. I now have a renewed passion to get this book's message to the masses, so, if you're reading this forward, thank you for your commitment to learning, for your drive to know about the health-wealth connection, and most importantly, for giving yourself permission to get in the driver's seat of your life plan.

My continued passion to reach women stems from my professional experiences. Since the release of the first and second editions, I've received feedback from both men and women about how relevant the information in this book is and how it has empowered women to take charge of their financial futures in a "female-friendly" manner. I have had the privilege of creating lifetime income plans and fully integrated life plans for individuals and families. I have presented hundreds of seminars, called "Total Well-Being," and I hear the same thing over and over. Women are looking to understand how they put together a financial blueprint that represents "more than the money;" a blueprint that integrates health needs and self-care, and treats these areas as equally important to taking care of your money. After all, one of the best ways to hold onto your wealth is to hold onto your health—a key premise of this book.

I have also recently released another book, "Planning a Purposeful Life: Secrets of Longevity," which was birthed from my desire to evolve my understanding of how to protect those I serve and how to help them live long, active, healthy, and purposeful lives. And, since you must have enough financial resources to live a long healthy life, it became quite apparent that I needed to get back to the basics, which are contained in this book. It's all about understanding the health-wealth connection, because check out the recent findings from a report released by the National Institute on Retirement Security in March of 2017 that should cause you to race to get your fully integrated life plan in place:

- Women overall are 80% more likely to be impoverished in retirement than men;
- Across all age groups, women have substantially less income in retirement than men;
- Women between the ages of 75 to 79 are three times more likely than men to be living in poverty;
- Widowed women are twice as likely to be living in poverty as their male counterparts; and
- Women who are widowed, divorced, and over age 70 rely on Social Security benefits for a majority of their income.

I didn't need this data to tell me why I need to continue reaching women and shouting from the mountaintops, encouraging women to take control of their financial lives. After all, I have a weekly Woman's Worth® radio program, and a week doesn't go by where I get a call from a frightened woman, typically in her mid- to late-70s, who calls me to get help because she is running out of money, wondering where she can go to get services. Or I get the frantic call from a woman who just realized her 32-year marriage was ending and she's only 53, or the widow who just retired to enjoy the journey with her husband and he suddenly passed away. I won't go further, but this recent data, coupled with our personal life realities, demands action. According to the U.S. Census Bureau, the fastest-growing decade of the U.S. population is 90-plus, and by 2050, reports show that there will be a million centenarians, many of whom, I would argue, are going to be women. That requires all of us as women—whether we're married, single, divorced, widowed—to step up our game of life and put as much energy into planning as we put into spending, or planning our next vacation or weekend getaway.

That's why you picked up this book, and if you already read an earlier edition, READ THIS ONE TOO! I did, and was renewed in my belief in my mission to help women balance their emotional, physical, and financial well-being through integrated life planning. After all ladies, It's more than the money! It's about TOTAL WELL-BEING! So, light a candle in your sacred space, pour a glass of your favorite beverage, relax, get a note pad and a highlighter, and enjoy the ride toward total well-being. I'd love to hear from you about your joyful ride toward total well-being, so feel free to reach out to me. And if you feel you need more guidance, particularly in the realm of finances, my contact information is at the back of the book. Give me a call, and I'll get you connected with a like-minded financial guide.

Introduction

Women, it is your birthright to be happy, healthy, and financially stable!

My name is Jeannette Bajalia, and I'm here to help you get there. No matter what you were taught growing up or what you'd like to believe, a man is not a plan when it comes to ensuring your financial stability. But you can claim that birthright by educating yourselves and taking control of your financial life and your money.

That's certainly not something I learned growing up. I'm the youngest of five girls; my parents immigrated, so I'm the first generation to grow up in the United States. My family's culture is one that says women don't need to be educated because we're just going to get married and be "supported by our husbands," so when I graduated from high school, the expectation was for me to simply get married and be taken care of by a husband. My sisters all got married and didn't pursue their college educations; my parents couldn't afford to put me through college, so I started working at Prudential the day after I graduated from high school with the intention of saving enough money to go to college. I started my career with the only thing I could do without having any education or many skills: I became a secretary, one of the primary career choices for women in 1969, when I graduated from high school. I was blessed with having a boss who saw that I had greater potential, and he started suggesting I move to different parts of the company. By the time I was 22 years old, I was in middle management. I realized that, in order to progress professionally, I needed to get a college education. I went to school at night while working full time, and earned my undergraduate degree in psychology.

Advancing my career at Prudential would have required that I leave sunny Florida and relocate to Newark, which I wasn't willing to do. So, after 13 years, I moved to another major corporation and spent 25 years there climbing the corporate ladder. It was during that time that I pursued my graduate education, again attending classes at night, and specializing in human resources. Even though I worked in various aspects of business, I always had a passion to focus on the human element, because it is through the people in a company that we improve the quality of our products and services. As a woman, I always got the more challenging assignments, the assignments that required me to sit there 60 and 70 hours a week, which were typically the assignments that my male colleagues didn't want.

I have spent more than 38 years of my adult life in corporate leadership and/or executive positions. I was always a pioneer — the first woman manager of this department, the first woman director of that department, the first woman to have achieved whatever rank I attained, pioneering my way through a corporate world that essentially looked at women as aliens.

As a woman in business, I learned very quickly there are significant differences in the way men and women process information, significant differences in communication styles, significant differences in expectations and work ethics; and so that was the world that socialized me, professionally. Climbing the corporate ladder, I reached a point where I realized I needed to do things quite differently to succeed. I wasn't willing to sell out to traditional attitudes, and I had a passion to help other women. Within the corporate setting, I was always coaching and mentoring other women because there weren't a lot of women in middle- and upper-management positions, so I helped them improve their effectiveness, learn new skills, and embrace a mindset that would contribute to their success. Most importantly, I coached them to be women — to not lose the femininity we are blessed with. I saw way too many women trying to compete with their male colleagues by taking on a male-oriented communication and leadership style. They wanted to run with the guys, and I found this quite distasteful as a younger, successful woman.

Now, let's add a bit more complexity and pressure to my life! At the age of 26, I became an instant caregiver after my father unexpectedly passed away. I not only became a caregiver, but I had to assume the full responsibility for the financial health and well-being of both a great-aunt and my mother — the experience opened my eyes. Basically, I saw all the cycles of caregiving, from emotional and physical care to financial care required for women as they journey through the various stages of their elder years. I didn't have children, but I had older women to take care of. So I transitioned my passion to be a mentor, supporting women in a corporate setting, and added to it a passion to be a caregiver in a family setting. I ended up caring for my mother and my aunt for more than 33 years of my adult life. My great-aunt lived to be over 100, and my mother lived to 93, and being with them gave me a whole new appreciation for the needs of women in the various life stages between the ages of 50 and 70, 70 and 80, 80 and 90, and beyond. One thing I quickly realized was that my parents never planned; they just kind of let things happen. That's how it happened that these two women ended up living on a Social Security check even below a poverty-level income. The greatest life lesson I learned at the age of 26 was to plan for the unknown. I had a choice to make when that unfortunate life event prematurely took away my hero and sidekick, my father. I could live in anger, frustration, and negative energy, which would define my future. Or I could take on the challenge with a positive, life-defining approach to ensure that this unexpected life event would position me for something much greater in the future. I opted for the latter, because I know God would never get me into something that He wouldn't get me through with dignity, grace, and strength.

The last nine years of my caregiving responsibilities were horrendous and quite eye-opening for me as a woman. They were rife with significant financial costs, as well as emotional costs. I did not acknowledge the fact that caregivers should give themselves permission to take a break, so I immersed myself in the care of my mother and lost myself in the process and the responsibilities. I was working more than 60 hours a week, and I'd come home and work another 60 hours a week on caring for my relatives, seven days a week. What became clear to me was that there weren't a lot of resources out there dedicated to helping seniors and, as important, helping caregivers. What I learned during my caregiving journey was that, when a person gets to be 80 or 90 years old, the medical and social systems just write them off. In this life stage, a person's medical, emotional, and financial needs are enormous, yet numerous professionals don't give the elderly quality care unless that older person has an advocate. Thus I became an advocate first for my mother and aunt, then for my mother's family members, and often for some of our elderly neighbors. With my new career, I am also an advocate for the men and women I serve in my financial practice. Seniors need advocates, but as long as they're able, they need to know how to be their own advocates. They need to take charge of their futures, whether with medical issues, financial issues or emotional issues. Seniors have to take charge of the most important stages of their lives to ensure total well-being — including the elder (or more mature) stages of life.

After my mother passed away, I continued trying to work in a career that I thought brought me great joy and a comfortable lifestyle, but I realized that what brought me joy was not my career — that was just a means to an end, and the end was the caregiving responsibility. My real purpose was ensuring a quality of life for those I loved and cared about. So, it was time in my life to search for a new purpose that was in alignment with my passions and my life experiences.

I made a commitment to myself: I was not going to repeat the cycle of depending on others for emotional and financial support from family, government, etc., and I wanted to shift my focus to helping women avoid being in poverty and avoid adding to the elderly poor statistics. I saw in my personal life and in my professional life that there was a common thread among women, and that was the significant impact of financial health on our physical and emotional health. As women, we're constantly living for today and we always want security, but we don't always have the discipline to create the plans to help us get from point A (where we are today) to point B (where we want to be in the future as we journey through life stages). Bottom line: I didn't want to be destitute when I was old, living merely on Social Security benefits, and I don't want other women to be destitute when they age, either. I feel that women should and can have vitality through the various stages of life by achieving an emotional, physical, and financial balance, and empowering themselves through information, education, and self-directed learning experiences.

After going through significant self-discovery and searching for my life's purpose after my caregiving responsibilities ended, I decided I was going to retire. I was 55 at the time. What helped me decide was participating in a mind, body, and spirit retreat in Italy. It was quite a stretch for me, and took me out of my comfort zone, but, to participate, I had to awaken a passion that I had suppressed within myself. I traveled and cycled eight days through Tuscany with a women's group I found on the internet. I needed to take some time to figure out what I wanted, and hoped to get some clarity. Was I ready to retire, or was it time to reinvent myself? It became very evident to me that I had outlived my usefulness in the corporate world, and that I had the desire to do something more purposeful, something that would impact the lives of individuals and families. Basically, I wanted to make sure that no individual or family was left in poor financial health when a loved one passed away or if they experienced an unexpected life event, whether it was due to the death of a spouse or partner, a divorce or any other life suddenness. I knew I wanted to work with seniors. I knew, too, that I wanted to work with women, and so I explored a variety of options.

I made the retirement decision at 55, which set me on another journey in trying to figure out how to manage my retirement assets. I needed help with my 401(k) and my pension plan, so I sought professional advice. I knew I had to answer questions such as:

- Should I take a lump-sum payout of my pension?
- How will I fund long-term care?
- How do I create an income plan from my retirement savings?
- How will I fund health care?
- How can I make sure I don't run out of money before I walk out on life?

There were numerous other issues that were even broader than the financial issues — they were life-planning issues. I talked to five different financial professionals and realized very quickly that they didn't really give a flip about me or my life goals. Basically, I wasn't relevant to them; my money was more relevant to them than I was. They just cared about getting their hands on my money, and they wanted me to go away and not ask questions. That wasn't going work for me, because I was determined to be in control of my future through my financial life plan — but they didn't want to help me in the way that I desired to be helped. It was going to be *their* plan, not *mine*; their way, or no way they would work with me. Two of the financial professionals I consulted decided they were going to screen me out because I was a single woman. I probed them about that and they said, "Well, typically, we have a minimum requirement of $500,000 of assets." As I listened to that, I was thinking, *Now, that's really ironic, because I have more than double that and these guys don't even act like they want to work with me.* I walked away feeling demoralized and undervalued.

I didn't get bitter; I realized that I could do what they could do, and I could help others in similar situations and bring more care and compassion into the financial services arena. I made a personal commitment and set a goal to do it even better, because I could put heart into the process and deal with more than the money; I would use a holistic approach. The day I walked out of that advisor's office, I made a life decision. I decided I would make it my life's mission to transform how women were served in the financial industry. No man, woman, individual, or family would experience what I experienced, and so my new mission and purpose was birthed.

First, I joined an estate and retirement planning firm, and helped the firm expand their products and services as the baby boomers were beginning their journey toward retirement. I wound up reinventing the firm and, ultimately, purchasing it from the man who'd hired me. I started building new models that addressed the specific needs of women: longevity issues, the fact that women usually have fewer financial resources, the fact that women spend so much of their time in caregiving roles. It was fascinating to see so many other women had gone through the same experience as me. To validate what I was seeing, I contracted with a national marketing firm in 2010, The Dalton Agency, headquartered in Jacksonville, Florida, to conduct two focus groups of single/divorced/widowed women, as well as married women who managed their family's finances, all in the 55 to 75 age group, to better understand women's attitudes toward financial matters. I was curious to learn what women thought about financial professionals and the services they were receiving, what they were expecting, what their primary needs were, and what their opinions were about investing and other financial and money matters. The Dalton Agency conducted two focus groups of around 25 randomly selected women, who had no knowledge of my firm prior to the discussions.

Half of the women we talked to were 55 to 65, and the other half were 65 to 75. The data from this focus group revealed important themes. Typically, these women:

- Desired to take a proactive and immediate approach to financial concerns such as investing, retirement, and protecting their futures, yet tended to be more risk-averse
- Wanted more security and guarantees not only for themselves but for their children
- Worried about affording health accommodations and assisted living facilities they might need in various life stages — long-term care was a big concern
- Wanted to protect not only their futures, but also the futures of their children and grandchildren
- Had no desire to be a burden on their children, and wanted their children to be able to maintain a certain standard of living after they're gone
- Had a great deal of uncertainty because of the many sources of information, advice, and opinions involving financial decisions
- Reported trouble learning about the options they had for investing and making right decisions
- Were adamant about their viewpoints around traits that make up a dependable financial professional and the specific qualities that create a positive or negative reputation

They also reported they had a high degree of fear and uncertainty — especially the divorced and widowed women, who found the economic climate was intimidating because, after years of being married, most of them realized their husbands had managed the finances in their lives. Further, they didn't trust financial professionals, and felt they were talked down to when they asked for information. Their responses validated what I was seeing, and that's how I birthed a second company, Woman's Worth®, to address the unique needs of women in the financial world using a more balanced approach that includes the physical, emotional, and financial components of life planning.

I didn't stop at my own focus group research; I continued to seek validation through other major research focused on what women want in financial services. My local findings were validated by a comprehensive survey conducted in 2009 by The Boston Consulting Group. The Group interviewed women around the world, and their findings were more of the same. Women around the world are more dissatisfied with financial services than any other industry that affects their daily lives. The Boston Consulting Group reported that many women believe their gender is a key factor in the disrespect and condescension they often experience and the poor advice they have received in the industry. Ah ha! My personal experience when I needed help was not unique, nor was the data I gathered from my local research. The financial industry UNDERSERVES us as women. My company, Woman's Worth®, and those advisors affiliated with my company have a unique and ever-so-compelling responsibility to help women pursue their life dreams and goals to and through the retirement journey.

I've learned some of the most amazing things on this journey, and have experienced consultations with women in various catastrophic life situations: recent widows, women who've just gone through terrible divorces, women betrayed by family members or business partners, all faced with having to make financial choices while on the point of emotional disaster. They talk about the kind of indifference, the lack of emotional connection or compassion they've encountered with male financial professionals.

I remember so vividly when a 50-year-old woman came to one of my educational seminars. As I was sharing stories about encouraging women to become more financially literate, I saw she was glassy-eyed and tearing up. She came to my office a few weeks later and shared her story.

At 48, she had been left a widow with a 12-year-old daughter. When she got married and she had their daughter, her husband convinced her to stay home even though she wanted to pursue a graduate degree and advance her career. She had an undergraduate degree, and she'd had a 12-year career in the Air Force, but he told her, "You don't have to worry about money. I will take care of you." Sound familiar? They had a nice lifestyle — she was raising their daughter and totally immersed herself in her parenting role — but guess what? He unexpectedly died. All of a sudden, he was gone, and she realized she knew nothing at all about their money. She was embarrassed to say she didn't know how to manage the finances. In her marriage, she was the caregiver and poured her entire energy store into her daughter and her daughter's life needs. She maintained the same financial advisor her husband had used, and shifted 100 percent of the financial management responsibility to him. Unfortunately, he saw fit to lose 50 percent of her portfolio during the Great Recession in 2008, because he didn't manage it any differently with her being a widow than he had when her husband had been alive and earning a fairly healthy and steady paycheck. Listening to her I realized, *I've got to reach out to these women. We have to turn this around. They're shifting their responsibility to others because they don't think they're smart enough or they're too embarrassed to say they don't know.*

So, I decided I needed to write this book, to reach out to women to communicate the message that we deserve better out of the financial industry. We are intelligent enough to be in control of our financial lives. With fact-based information communicated in a manner that we speak, not "male-speak," we can feel empowered to make the right financial choices that enable us to achieve our life goals in a personal, customized manner, as unique to us as women as our very own divinely created PLAN. We have to know how to ask the people who are helping us the right questions, and hold them accountable to help us in the manner that we need to be helped — not in the manner they think we should be helped.

Balance is everything, and you can't really enjoy health, wealth or emotional stability without keeping a focus on all these aspects of life. None of those things can stand alone. You probably get a physical exam every year, but regular emotional and financial checkups are just as important. Knowledge is power; I've seen far too many women being taken advantage of, their nest eggs plundered, or who compromise the quality of their lives because they've ignored the need to achieve the right balance between their emotional, physical, and financial health.

As I progressed in pursuit of my aim to advance my life planning models to help women more effectively and in the manner they desire, I realized there was just nothing in the financial industry that put these three key areas — health, wealth, and emotional balance — together, because most people in the financial world cared and focused on the financial element, period. They wanted you to go away and let them take care of your money. It was the same in other areas. In the physical realm, doctors more or less practice medicine by treating you as a series of independent body systems, not as a whole person. In the emotional realm, the notion seemed to be that women who hit 50 and were experiencing menopause were crazy and could not think rationally.

I saw this very disconnected process and the detrimental impact it had on women, and realized I needed to bring all this together and send a message. The key to vitality for women lies in physical, emotional, and financial balance; it's up to us to seek it out and to empower ourselves through knowledge, through information, and through connections with like-minded women. It's up to us to align ourselves with a team of professionals, like-minded people who can help us stay in balance and be facilitators of our life plans. Most importantly, as women, we should give ourselves permission to focus on "self-care."

We're really the first generation of women who have had to think about this stuff. The baby boomers are the first generation that has enjoyed a healthy middle class that had any wealth, and now, for the first time in our nation, 51 percent of the wealth is in the hands of women — with that number only expected to grow.[1] Yet, many of the women poised to take on this wealth were never taught how to deal with wealth as a means to an end, or as the means to each woman's own end of having a purposeful life and attaining her own goals and dreams. As I mentioned previously, I was raised in a traditional environment, where the message that I got was to go out and find a man to take care of me for the rest of my life. So I had to relearn my social conditioning, just as many women will often do after a major life event.

One thing I've learned through both my business and personal experiences is that a man is not a plan. Let's wake up and take charge. We want financial health, and to have that we need to ensure our physical and emotional health are in balance, too. We have to anticipate and prepare for a long life, much longer than previous generations could expect, and that means taking care of all three aspects of total health.

---

[1] Ryan Gorman. Business Insider. April 7, 2015. "Women now control more than half of US personal wealth, which 'will only increase in years to come'." http://www.businessinsider.com/women-now-control-more-than-half-of-us-personal-wealth-2015-4. Accessed Feb. 28, 2017.

Now, I wouldn't describe myself as a liberated woman, and I believe in traditional family values. However, I do recognize that when women are mobilized to take charge of their future, powerful things happen. When we take charge of our future through our social connections with other women who complement what we know and don't know, we can protect and preserve the quality of our senior years, because we're the gender that has more potential to live to be over 100 years old. When we work with our spouses or partners in making mutual financial decisions that achieve our mutual goals, we become more confident, should we have a tragic life event.

Women's lives have always been about others: their husbands, partners, children, aging parents, all of their caregiving responsibilities. We have to have the tools to help ourselves, and the will to say, "This is about *me*." I pray that, as you read this book, the spirit of life, purpose, and passion will ignite in you and encourage you to take action, because, ladies, *it's more than the money*! It's about your total well-being and your financial independence.

Checking Up on Your Financial Health

CHAPTER ONE

Women Are Different From Men – and Not Just in the Ways You Think

"If you're given a choice between money and sex appeal, take the money. As you get older, the money will become your sex appeal."
– Katherine Hepburn

Women and men are different on many levels, but the ones I want to talk about here pertain to retirement challenges. There are compelling statistics that drive the differences: women are 27 percent more likely than men to have NO retirement savings.[2]

Here are some other fascinating facts to consider:

- On average, a woman's earnings are $0.79 to every $1 a man has earned, and that translates to about a $430,000 lifetime loss.[3]

---

[2] Elyssa Kirkham. GoBankingRates. March 14, 2016. "1 in 3 Americans Have $0 Saved for Retirement." https://www.gobankingrates.com/retirement/1-3-americans-0-saved-retirement/. Accessed Feb. 28, 2017.

- More than 70% of nursing home residents are women; this fact has significant financial impact. [4]
- 40% percent of women age 65 or older are widows. [5]
- Women are 80% more likely to be impoverished in retirement. [6]
- 50% of marriages end up in divorce, and today in America the average age of widowhood is 56. [7]
- On average, a woman spends 12 years in various unpaid caregiving roles, resulting in a lifetime financial loss experts estimate to be more than $320,000. [8]
- If you consider the collective sum of reduced salary AND reduced retirement benefits, caregivers lose $659,139 over a lifetime. [9]

---

[3] Kaitlin Holmes and Danielle Corley. Center for American Progress. April 12, 2016. "The Top 10 Facts About the Gender Wage Gap." https://www.americanprogress.org /issues/women/reports/2016/04/12/135260/the-top-10-facts-about-the-gender-wage-gap/. Accessed Feb. 28, 2017.

[4] American Association for Long-Term Care Insurance. "Long-Term Care - Important Information for Women." http://www.aaltci.org/long-term-care-insurance/ learning-center/for-women.php. Accessed Feb. 28, 2017.

[5] Richard Eisenberg. July 1, 2014. "Who Are Americans 65 and Older?" https://www.forbes.com/sites/nextavenue/2014/07/01/who-are-americans-65-and-older/#a4b4cfd3fdb4. Accessed Feb. 28, 2017.

[6] National Institute on Retirement Security. March 1, 2016. "Women 80% More Likely to be Impoverished in Retirement." http://www.nirsonline.org/index.php?option =content&task=view&id=913. Accessed Feb. 28, 2017.

[7] Illinois Department of financial & Professional Regulation. 2015. "Financial Literacy – Retirement: Widow/Divorce." https://www.idfpr.com/finlit101/Retirement /widow.asp. Accessed Feb. 28, 2017.

[8] Family Caregiver Alliance. February 2015. "Who Are the Caregivers?" https://www.caregiver.org/women-and-caregiving-facts-and-figures. Accessed Feb. 28, 2017.

[9] National Center on Women and Aging and the National Alliance for Caregivers. The MetLife Juggling Act. New York, NY. 1999

Now, let's add to these compelling statistics and facts that 80 percent of men die married, while 80 percent of women die single. That means that most assuredly, the majority of women will find themselves in a primary financial decision-making role at some point in their lives.[10] Can you begin to see why women are at greater financial risk in retirement, in what should be their golden years?

Ninety percent of women will be responsible for managing their money at some point in their lives.[11] Traditionally in marriages, the household budget responsibilities are left to the woman, but the investment responsibilities and the planning responsibilities are typically the husband's. That means that this 90 percent is going to have a pretty steep learning curve when the responsibility passes on to them.

One study revealed some pretty interesting statistics about women in retirement. Here are some amazing facts from that study:[12]

- 56% of women plan to work into their elder years.
- 64% of baby boomer women don't have a backup plan if they are forced into early retirement.
- 29% plan to rely on Social Security or welfare.

---

[10] Family Wealth Advisors Council. BusinessWire. Aug. 18, 2015. "New Study Reveals What Women Breadwinners Want and Need and How They Are 'Leaning In' on Financial Decisions." http://www.businesswire.com/news/home/20150818005413/en/CORRECTING-REPLACING-Study-Reveals-Women-Breadwinners-%E2%80%9CLeaning. Accessed April 25, 2017.

[11] Dominique Mosbergen. The Huffington Post. Aug. 14, 2017. "The Gender Gap that No One's Talking About." http://www.huffingtonpost.com/entry/financial-wellness-literacy-gender-gap_us_578dcf76e4b0c53d5cfabc3f. Accessed Feb. 28, 2017.

[12] TransAmerica Center for Retirement Studies. March 1, 2016. "16 Facts that Illustrate Women's Risky Retirement Prospects." https://www.transamericacenter.org/docs/default-source/women-and-retirement/tcrs2016_pr_womens_retirement_outlook.pdf. Accessed Feb. 28, 2017.

- Among women who have planned for retirement income, the majority, 62%, "guessed" at their income needs.

Not surprisingly, only 12 percent of women included in the study say they are "very confident" in their ability to retire with a comfortable lifestyle. And, judging by these statistics, they may well be right.

A woman who has not been diagnosed with a life-threatening illness by the age of 65 today has life expectancy of more than 20 years,[13] and that has some significant financial implications. One of the more worrisome statistics is the cost of all the unpaid care-giving women experience in their lifetimes, and its impact on their Social Security benefits. Women are typically the ones who step out of the workforce to take care of their children, to take care of aging family members, sick relatives, sick spouses, and even friends, because the men walk out on life first. Women usu-ally outlive their husbands and take care of them until they die, which is why 70 percent of nursing home residents are women. Additionally, from what I have observed in my practice, women who haven't done adequate planning for retirement income typi-cally use up all their resources in caregiving for their husbands and then live out the rest of their days not even in individual private nursing facilities but in Medicaid nursing homes.

Here are some statistics about caregiving. According to the Na-tional Alliance for Caregiving and AARP, there are 43.5 million adults in the United States who are providing care to a relative or a friend. Of those caregivers, 60 percent are women.[14]

---

[13] Social Security Administration. "Actuarial Life Table: 2013 Period Life Table." https://www.ssa.gov/oact/STATS/table4c6.html. Accessed Feb. 28, 2017.

[14] National Alliance for Caregiving. AARP. June 2015. "2015 Report: Caregiving in the U.S." http://www.aarp.org/content/dam/aarp/ppi/2015/caregiving-in-the-united-states-2015-report-revised.pdf. Accessed Feb. 28, 2017.

Remember that earlier we said caregivers lost about $320,000 in lifetime earnings as a result of their caregiving responsibilities? And that represents the lost income only from stepping out of the workforce; when you add the loss of retirement benefits, the opportunity cost is closer to $659,000 across a caregiver's lifetime. I know the rude reality of that from my personal experience. That loss has significant implications for women, given their disproportionate numbers as caregivers.

The good news for women in the U.S.: as cited before, for the first time, American women hold the majority share of the country's private wealth; about $14 trillion.[15] Unfortunately, while they have the responsibility for their own ever-increasing wealth management, women consistently report that they don't feel confident in their ability to deal with financial matters. As there will be more transference of wealth in the next decade, it's projected that women will hold closer to $22 trillion by 2020. Yet the financial models that we're using are not taking into consideration the factors I talked about earlier, and the unique challenges that face women: longevity issues requiring funding active lifestyles for longer periods, lower earnings, fewer pension plans, and the fact they suffer more debilitating illnesses than the male gender.

Our lives as women are changing. As we are living longer than our mothers and grandmothers did, we are reinventing ourselves well into our 60s and 70s. I have a client who is 83 years old and is out on the tennis court twice a week, thanks to a knee replacement and a hip replacement. And she's not alone; women are staying more active and more vibrant. They have more vitality through the various stages of life during the golden years (or as I

---

[15] Ryan Gorman. Business Insider. April 7, 2015. "Women now control more than half of US personal wealth, which 'will only increase in years to come'." http://www.businessinsider.com/women-now-control-more-than-half-of-us-personal-wealth-2015-4. Accessed Feb. 28, 2017.

like to put it, the more mature years). They're just not ready to roll up and call themselves retired. Many boomer women are reinventing themselves once they "retire" from their primary professions or roles in life, and are "rewiring" themselves into more purposeful lives. Having money is important in enabling us to have a quality lifestyle during the various phases of the latter part of our lives. But it isn't just about having money for the purpose of saying your bank account is healthy; that money represents a means to an end with the end being the achievement of your dreams, your goals, or for whatever purpose you spent a lifetime accumulating your money.

Ken Dychtwald is a researcher, a speaker, and an educator in the area of retirement and life stages and focuses his studies on what's happening to our society as it matures. He created a life-stage model that reflects the changing lifestyle we're seeing as we live longer and healthier lives. The stage from 25 to 40 is called young adulthood. From 40 to 60, it's called "middlescence." Sixty to 80 is adulthood. In the past, the 60-to-80 crowd was considered to be old age, but old age now is 60 to 100, and 100-plus is very old age. Isn't that good news, ladies? I like it, since I am simply in my adulthood and already retired from my first career and have spent the last 10 years creating my "purposeful career." Looks like many of us will have two or three careers before we can actually call ourselves "retired." In fact, we should all take the word "retirement" out of our vocabulary. It's all about reinventing yourself into a more purposeful lifestyle that you create, not one created out of default in a professional career that may or may not have been out of financial necessity.

These new life stages ring true to what I have seen in my practice. They require us to make a fundamental shift from retirement planning to lifestyle planning, because we have to plan for our lifelong savings, our nest egg, to get us through the 60-to-80, the 80-to-100, and 100-plus life stages, and financial models are not taking all these life-stage needs into consideration. I've seen the numbers; traditional, statistical models are just knocking people off at the age of 90, and I'm wondering, *What are they thinking?* I've got several clients who are still taking care of their mothers who are in their late 90s.

Where should the money to support our later lifestyles be coming from? Typically, 39 percent of your lifestyle income comes from Social Security; yet I see women try to live 100 percent on Social Security. It won't work; according to the Social Security Administration, Social Security was never intended to be the sole source of a retiree's lifestyle income. Eighteen percent of lifestyle income might come from some type of pension plan, and the other 43 percent could come from personal savings and investments. The traditional model of Social Security being our primary retirement income is absolutely archaic and needs to be tossed, because it represents less than 40 percent of the income that we'll need.

If you remember the statistics we looked at earlier, one of them was that women earn $0.79 to every $1.00 that men earn, and that most women are in jobs that don't have pension plans. This validates the fact that we must find some unique planning approaches and models to help women make up that difference, so they don't end up in the elderly poor population. To avoid becoming a member of this population, we need to improve our financial literacy, take charge of our financial future, get our heads out of the sand, and start saving and investing, even well into our elder years. We may not have done it in our 30s and 40s, but we've got to start doing it in our 50s and 60s.

Given that we're staying more active, too, we have to go beyond planning for the basic expenses and plan also to cover the costs of our interests, hobbies, and passions. And, for women, for self-care due to longevity because we need to make sure we hold on to our wealth by holding on to our health. Recently I was working with a newly retired client, creating her retirement income strategy. She was in her early 60s. I asked her, "What are the things that you want to pursue?"

With men you typically hear, "I want to play golf two times a week," or, "I need a thousand dollars a month to take my boat out and go fishing." This particular client said, "I have had a passion for art and I have never been able to pursue it, because everything went to the kids and toward getting them through college. Now I want to take art classes, and I want to be able to buy art supplies." Well, art supplies aren't cheap, so we created a budget for art education and supplies.

There has to be funding for special interests like hers, because living well and holistically is about the whole person. It's not just about your financial life; it's also about the quality of your emotional and physical life. That's why those special interests need to be tied to the funds: it is essential to our well-being to have the resources to pursue our desires and passions. It keeps us healthier longer, and if we are going to live longer, we need to live those years with abundant health and with wealth.

Also, what's often overlooked with regard to women are medical and health care costs that go beyond what Medicare is going to provide. Over the next five years, with health care reform, the budget deficit, and the budget reduction plans that our infamous Congress is working through, I believe we are going to see Social Security reform and Medicare reforms that will impact both men and women, but women more so, due to the longevity factor. Women have more to lose, because more than likely, the regulators will change the formula for calculating Social Security, since women are living so much longer. The financial industry has typically had a mantra that would say something like: "your greatest risk to your retirement is inflation, taxes, and market volatility." Well, sound the alarm, as I'm here to suggest to you that, as a woman, your greatest risk is the skyrocketing costs of routine medical care. So, it would behoove you to build into your life and financial plans all those out-of-pocket costs that could throw you a curve ball as you are journeying through what should be your purposeful retirement.

Additionally, long-term-care expenses are often not considered with regard to women. There needs to be a balance for married couples and for those in any type of partnership where you manage your lives jointly; couples need to protect themselves from spending down all their retirement assets on the care of one of the spouses at the expense of the other.

There's long been a myth in retirement planning that all you need to plan for when you retire is 70 percent of the average income that you had the last five years of your employment. The truth of the matter is that, because of the rising cost of health care, the chances of women living into their late 90s or early 100s, and their desires to retain active lifestyles for longer time periods (yes, we could still be traveling into our late 80s and 90s!), we have to work toward a higher goal. What it's looking like, when you project out the needs of women through their elder years, is that they may actually need to plan for significantly more, perhaps closer to 135 percent, of the income they had when they were working. Again, it's those longevity issues and the costs associated with unanticipated health care crises that will mean more out-of-pocket expenses, because we're likely to see health care costs being shifted increasingly to the consumer in the next decade. We have to start planning today for the possibility of that. And if it never happens, then we'll have a more joyful life, because we'll have more money to spend; or, as many women consistently tell me, you can leave some money to the kids and grandkids as a legacy that will be appreciated and cherished over the years.

While those statistics are really distressing, they're also quite motivating, because information empowers us to take action. Without that action, you can't do much.

The bottom line is that your happiness matters, and your health depends upon it. You need a proper life plan that creates a retirement income plan distributed to you monthly, like clockwork, in a predictable way, one that covers the maintenance of physical and emotional well-being, and that retains the integrity of your financial well-being.

Now, let's move on to discuss simple strategies and ideas to get you on the journey toward your new and more certain future — the golden nuggets for your golden and more mature years.

CHAPTER TWO

Your Legacy Documents

"When planning for a year, plant corn. When planning for a decade, plant trees. When planning for a lifetime, train and educate people."
– Chinese Proverb

I am not an attorney. Yet, every day I meet with women and families who are concerned for their legacies. More than getting through retirement, they worry about family members who will come after them, and about preserving their hard work and its impact, and essentially protecting their beneficiaries from themselves, from making unwise financial choices should they come upon an inheritance. So, while I don't provide legal services or advice, I'd like to help you familiarize yourself with the different kinds of estate planning and preparation documents that you might encounter, and encourage you to pursue the issue with the help of both your financial professional and a qualified estate planning attorney.

First and foremost, the most important thing women need to do to protect and preserve what they worked very hard to accumulate is ensure that they have the proper legal documents. Maybe all you own is your house, but you still want to protect your home. You also want to ensure ease of estate distribution to your loved ones, should something happen to you unexpectedly. Life throws us curve balls quite suddenly, so you'll need to be prepared "just in case" you get one of these curve balls.

Remember, ladies, "estate" is not synonymous with wealth. Far too often, we don't feel like we need an estate plan because we don't have a lot of money. This is a myth we need to dispel immediately. I am not an estate planning attorney, but legacy planning is critical as part of your life planning because you'll want to have your financial matters organized once you're gone. And, from personal experience, I can tell you, there are certain typical problems that without proper advance planning can create a burden on those we leave behind. For most women, their greatest desire is to leave a legacy and to not be a burden on their children or their husbands — not to create a mess when they take that limousine to heaven. Yet, 58 percent of Americans are missing critical legacy and estate planning documents.[16] And you want to make sure, if you do have estate planning documents, they are compliant with current day estate laws at the state level and federal level, because laws do change.

What are some of the financial burdens your heirs could face if you don't plan properly? There are lots of fees involved in probate, and the costs can be high. There are CPA fees, attorney fees, and probate court costs. Other estate settlement costs are state and federal death taxes, which apply to estates that exceed certain amounts. Death tax exclusions change, based on regulations. Currently, through 2017, the limit is set at $5.49 million a person, so a

---

[16] Maurie Backman. USA Today as reprinted from The Motley Fool. Feb. 21, 2017. "58% of Americans are making this huge retirement mistake." http://www.usatoday.com/story/money/personalfinance/retirement/2017/02/21/58-of-americans-are-making-this-huge-retirement-mistake/97819214/. Accessed March 1, 2017.

couple can protect $11 million with the proper legal documents.[17] But we have seen estate tax exclusions lower than $250,000 in just the last 40 years,[18] so estate tax settlement can be a big financial burden. I don't know about you, but I want to see my money go to those I love and care about, *not* to the government.

Because of improper planning, heirs sometimes have to shoulder the burden of the expenses of settling an estate before they've gotten a dime from it. When someone dies suddenly, there may not be enough liquid assets immediately available to pay estate settlement costs. I have even seen situations in which a family has to go out of pocket to cover funeral expenses, because the estate is tied up in probate. I recently met with a woman who was appointed by the probate court to act as her brother's personal representative because he died without a will. Unfortunately, he and his family died in a plane crash that her brother was piloting. She reported to me that, 10 years after the passing of her brother and his family, she was still in probate because her brother had multiple properties, financial accounts, and a lot of leases and such on both residential and commercial properties. Much of this could have been avoided with a proper legacy plan. But then, her brother was only 45 and likely never expected to walk out on life so soon.

Another problem is cash flow, specifically when there's not enough income to care for the loved ones left behind: the spouse or partner and the minor children. Bad planning can mean some nasty surprises when you lose your spouse or partner, like the loss of employment income, a pension check, or a Social Security

---

[17] Ashlea Ebeling. Forbes. Oct. 25, 2016. "IRS Announces 2017 Estate and Gift Tax Limits: The $11 Million Tax Break." https://www.forbes.com/sites/ashleaebeling/2016/10/25/irs-announces-2017-estate-and-gift-tax-limits-the-11-million-tax-break/#2b92c5813b70. Accessed March 1, 2017.

[18] Tax Foundation. Feb. 4, 2014. "Federal Estate and Gift Tax Rates, Exemptions and Exclusions 1916-2014." https://taxfoundation.org/federal-estate-and-gift-tax-rates-exemptions-and-exclusions-1916-2014/. Accessed March 16, 2017.

check. A good plan should prevent you from being surprised when all of a sudden you're living on 30 percent less income a month, because there's only one Social Security check, or only 50 percent — or zero! — of a pension benefit left.

Another issue is the ability to transfer assets; obviously estates are subject to probate delays and significant expenses. Will you be leaving assets to a minor child? Often, those assets go into guardianship accounts until the child attains age 18, or in some states 21, and would typically be distributed outright to the heirs, which can be risky. Do you want assets distributed outright without controls? What about heirs who are on some type of government assistance due to a disability? These types of family issues call for what are commonly referred to as "special needs" provisions in legal documents.

There could be additional taxes and estate expenses that will be paid out if there was inadequate pre-death planning. It's very important for individuals who are holding IRAs or any tax-deferred retirement accounts to ensure that those assets are held with the right institution, one that allows you to stretch those retirement accounts to your loved ones without having to be paid out immediately or within five years, as is typically required if the retirement accounts are still held within an employer-sponsored plan in the form of 401(k)s, deferred-compensation plans, or 403(b)s and such. Some custodians of employer-sponsored plans may not provide stretch provisions. Stretch provisions for individual retirement accounts are strategies you can use create family wealth across multiple generations and leave a legacy to your loved ones. You'll need to understand the distribution rules associated with retirement accounts which cannot be jointly held.

Another pitfall you can avoid with proper legal documents is poor asset management, which can happen if the wrong person is chosen to manage the assets left to your minor children or grandchildren. Even adult children many times can't always handle their inheritance wisely. They may be having financial challenges and could be facing bankruptcy, claims from lawsuits, creditors, etc. They might be having gambling issues, or they might have a drinking or drug problem, and cannot manage the assets that they get, so those assets need to be put in a trust for them in order to protect them from their own poor decision making.

There are many issues that arise when transferring assets at death that need to be thought through before they become costly to your family. I've seen situations where 45 to 65 percent of estates are lost to taxes and avoidable costs because of poor legal planning of the estate, and I'm of the opinion I don't want to give the government one penny more than they deserve. I'll share my favorite line from my CPA here: "Render unto Caesar what is Caesar's — but don't give him any of yours!"

Things that you should consider in your estate planning are:

- How to protect your personal property: your houses, your cars, your vacation home. A lot of people forget their timeshares when tallying up their assets.
- How to protect your retirement plan: your stocks, bonds, investment accounts, insurance policies and contracts, annuity contracts, and all business interests.
- How to protect your heirs from themselves: preserving their disability benefits and protecting their inheritance from being squandered because of their bad judgment or habits, rocky marriages, etc.

What are the types of fees that nip away at the estate? In addition to the aforementioned death taxes, accounting fees, and legal fees, you have appraisal fees, because if your children are going to inherit your home, they'll have to have the value of it at the time of death so they can get the stepped-up basis (the current value of the home rather than the purchase price of the home), which is a benefit to your heirs. Added to that can be executor's or trustee's fees, when appropriate. All of these factors should be taken into consideration, and proper planning can minimize the costs associated with them, so your loved ones get to keep more.

There are various types of legal documents an individual needs, and I'd like to dispel the notion of one-size-fits-all that I hear so often. Many of my clients go to seminars, then come and tell me, "Everybody needs a living trust." That's just not true. Many people simply need a will and some powers of attorney to protect them, because they don't have anything to put in the trust, and a trust is valid only if it's funded with assets.

There are various types of wills and trusts to fit the needs of the individual, and determining the proper legal documents for your situation hinges upon your being clear about your desires: what are your preferences, and what do you want for your loved ones on the day that you walk out of life?

Let's start with the most common document: a will. The type of will you see most often is often called an "I love you" will: a basic, simple will that generally gives everything outright to the surviving spouse or the children without rules or restrictions.

There is a will with a contingent trust, because frequently married couples with minor children will pass everything to the surviving spouse or partner, if they're living, and if not it can go into trust for minor children until they become adults. So a will can have a provision to create a trust to accomplish what you desire.

Then you have what are called "pour-over" wills. The pour-over will is used in conjunction with a living trust. Basically what the pour-over will does is pick up any assets that were not transferred to the trust during the person's lifetime and pour them over into the trust upon death. These assets will go into probate, but the terms and conditions of the trust determine the distribution. It's another safety protection. Here's an example of how that works: say that I opened up a $50,000 CD in my name; then I died, and all my other financial accounts were in my trust. They were all titled to my trust, except this one CD. Well, the pour-over will says that the CD really belongs to the trust, so when it goes to probate, it will be distributed in accordance with the trust provisions. Whatever the desires of the deceased person were, as described in their trust, those apply also to this $50,000 CD. It goes through probate because it's not titled to the trust, but it's simple probate, not a drawn-out probate process.

There's also another legal document, appropriate for some situations, called a revocable living trust without any limitations that would not restrict use of the estate's assets. Generally, this means that the surviving spouse has full control of the principal and income of the estate. The main purpose of a living trust is to avoid probate. If it's required, the trust can also be used to manage the assets of beneficiaries who aren't ready to inherit the assets outright because they lack financial experience or investment experience, or because they're just not mature enough, or because they've got other issues that mean you don't want to give them a full distribution. You can spell out in the trust what your specific desires are for the distribution of the estate and how that is going to be handled.

Then there's another form of a living trust often used for estates of higher value, which is also called a credit shelter or AB trust. It's just a living trust with a credit shelter provision, which avoids probate and also makes certain that both spouses use the actual estate tax credit or exclusion amount. For instance, a credit shelter trust says that, if the estate tax exemption is $5 million this year, then if I have a credit shelter trust, I can have $5 million and my spouse can have $5 million, so when the first person dies I can protect that full $10 million. The federal estate tax limits are adjusted for inflation annually.

If there is a large life insurance policy in the estate that may put the estate at risk for death taxes — because it will put the estate over the exclusion — you and your attorney may decide to create what we call an irrevocable life insurance trust, which is simply a gift trust. It keeps that life insurance out of the estate so you can minimize estate taxes. While life insurance is income-tax free, it is not estate-tax free if it exceeds the limit once added to the total value of the estate.

The determination of whether you need a will or a trust is a function of the size of the estate, what you're trying to accomplish, and your personal life situation. It requires a complete assessment of what your life situation is while you're alive, what you can anticipate happening when you're not here, and how to best protect your heirs from all those unique situations and life circumstances.

The purpose of wills and trusts is to keep the probate costs managed and/or totally eliminated. Additionally, a trust offers a way to distribute your estate in as timely and cost-efficient a manner as possible.

Other key legal documents are called powers of attorney. The first one I'm going to talk about is the durable power of attorney, a document that one person, known as the "principal," uses to empower another person (the "attorney in fact"), to hold the power to act on his or her behalf. I am a competent adult and I have established a durable power of attorney. If I have some type of temporary incapacity that renders me unable to pay my mortgage, or if I'm unable to write checks, or if I'm unable to make decisions about my financial or business affairs, then my assigned attorney in fact has the right to speak on my behalf and sign on my behalf. Some of the powers that are included in this, for instance, would be buying, selling, or releasing assets, suing someone to protect the principal, collecting from creditors, changing provisions of a living trust if we know it needs to be changed, or operating my business affairs. There are other powers, too: you can make gifts to a spouse or grandchildren. You can take action and get the proper legal documents to support whatever that event requires or whatever changes are necessitated. Basically, a durable power of attorney assigns the power to exercise special powers in financial matters.

As mentioned previously, you should frequently have a "power of attorney check-up," because laws change and, when there is a need in your life, you want to make sure your power of attorney is up to date and follows any necessary regulations. As I write this, I'm reminded of a woman who came to one of my workshops. Her father had just had a stroke and couldn't make his financial decisions anymore and she wanted to know how to get him a power of attorney. Unfortunately, she needed some legal and court interventions to make this happen, and it took time and jumping through hoops for her to be able to make financial decisions on his behalf. Estate planning is a required discipline in your life plan, so give it the serious attention needed to help protect you and your loved ones.

There are different kinds of powers of attorney. Again, which of them you choose is a function of what your specific situation may be. There is a general power of attorney, which gives the holder all of the powers possessed by the principal, so that everything I have along with all of my powers are transferred to my attorney in fact. On the other hand, there could be special powers of attorney with limits that would be specified in your power of attorney. So it's important to ensure that the durable power of attorney represents what your desires are, and, as important, that it is compliant with the laws of the state in which they will be exercised. Also, it's worth noting here that you should be thoughtful about who you select as your designated attorney in fact. Just because you have a son or daughter, or another family member or friend, they may not have the mindset or the ability to make the right financial choices on your behalf. Look at their financial lives and that will give you a clue as to how they might handle your financial matters.

You may also want to have a health care power of attorney in place. This could be an especially important consideration for family members over the age of 18, because if you have children away at college and they have a medical situation, you need a power of attorney in place to get information about their medical situation. For privacy reasons, you cannot receive personal health information about an adult — even your adult son or daughter — without this document in place. A health care power of attorney gives you that right, and makes it possible for you to navigate through the health care system to be able to access medical records and talk to medical professionals, and to help you exercise the choices that need to be made from a medical perspective. Most of us don't even know what prescription medications our spouses take, but in the event of an emergency situation, you need a health care power of attorney for your spouse to empower you to get that information from the doctor. If you are helping your parents navigate through the health care system, you're not going to be able to do it without having health care power of attorney, particularly updated health care power of attorney, because in 2005, HIPAA compliance changed, which required certain language in health care powers of attorney. Eighty percent of the individuals I meet with have old, outdated health care powers of attorney. These documents don't work on your behalf if they're outdated, so make sure that yours are up-to-date and are reviewed frequently. As important, make sure you have the right person designated as your attorney in fact, and that there are alternates identified should your first designated person not be able to fulfill his or her responsibilities.

I caution women in second marriages to ensure that they talk as a couple about these matters. I recently met with a widow who was not the trustee of her husband's trust. He had assured her she would be taken care of should he pass on, but he died unexpectedly, and now she has to go through a trustee to get income and request any money beyond typical living expenses. Ladies, this is not where you want to be. He thought he was taking care of her, but in fact he had inadvertently added to the complexities of her financial future, as she is required to go through a third party to access her funds.

Then we have the living will. Many individuals try to include their end-of-life wishes in their health care power of attorney. You want to discuss this with your attorney, who may advise you to keep these two things totally separate, because you need a living will to be more explicit, and the health care power of attorney comes into play when you're still alive and can still speak for yourself. The living will comes in when it has been deemed by your doctors that you are in the final stage of life, and that there is no chance of recovery. It allows you to exercise your constitutional rights for how you want to be treated medically when the end is near. Do you want to be on a respirator? Do you want to be resuscitated if you're 85 years old and you've got terminal cancer and you go into heart failure? Do you want a feeding tube? Do you want to be treated by a certain type of medical professional? Do you want experimental treatment? This document comes into play at the point at which you actually can't speak for yourself and there's no likelihood that you're going to recover, so having that living will in place to speak for you is important. The Hospice Foundation of America (www.hospicefoundation.org) has a document called "The Instruments of Advance Care Planning" on their website that explains in detail what the legal requirements and documents are that you should have in place. Also, through the nonprofit organization Aging with Dignity you can get access to an informative and helpful booklet on these topics called "Five Wishes" by ordering it through www.agingwithdignity.org or calling (888) 5-WISHES to purchase this guide. In many states, the Five Wishes document is accepted as a health care power of attorney, as well as in place of a living will, but you need to check with your estate planning attorney to validate your specific state requirements.

Let's talk a little about the differences between a will versus a trust, since this seems to create a bit of confusion. All wills go through probate in the state the death occurred. But assuming you have a correctly drawn-up will, it's not a lengthy and expensive process, and 100 percent of your estate will go through probate with a will. A will is the legal instrument used for probate. Wills are public documents. Everybody and their brother can go to the clerk of court in the county of death and get a copy of your will. When Elizabeth Edwards died, I did a Google search and pulled up her will. The same thing is true of the courts' declaration of who will be appointed as the trustee for Prince's estate, because he died without a will. I can get a will from anyone: a copy of Anna Nicole Smith's will arrived on our office fax machine, unsolicited. You'll need to understand if you're okay with this type of public information on your estate and your beneficiaries.

Trusts, on the other hand, are private, personal documents. None of your estate has to go through probate if everything is titled to your trust — only those assets that were not titled to the trust. With a trust, you can easily transfer assets to your heirs without the complications of probate. A trust saves attorneys' fees, executors' fees, and many other potential professional management fees. Most important, it saves precious time.

Estate planning attorneys can create these legal documents— but it's important to remember that estate planning attorneys are not financial professionals; nor are they planners. They do a good job of getting you legally protected, but what I find very often is that while individuals are very quick to get a trust established and executed, they don't go to the next step. What makes a trust legitimate is that there are some assets attached to the trust, which is called funding your trust. Many people establish living trusts to avoid probate and administration costs, to reduce their death taxes, and to manage assets for any minor children or any unique situations in their family, but too frequently these trusts are completely unfunded: The assets are still titled to the individual and not to the name of the trust. People forget to transfer their home to the trust as well, if appropriate. They neglect to transfer brokerage accounts, checking accounts, or the deed to the vacation home, so the benefits of having a trust in the first place are lost. It's important to validate that all of your necessary assets have been titled to your trust, because any assets not specifically named will have to go through probate. These assets without any beneficiary attached to them, as in a "payable on death," include savings accounts, checking accounts, any money market accounts, any brokerage accounts, corporate stock, and any CDs, as well as any general partnership that you have in a business. Your life insurance policy beneficiary can be the trust or an individual, or it may need to go into another kind of trust. Real estate generally is transferred to the trust by having the attorney prepare the new deed, but this step has to be considered based on what you want to happen to the home. Also, often I find that clients fail to title deeds to timeshare properties to the trust, so remember to check that timeshare deeds are titled to your trust when you work on funding your trust.

Which assets won't go into the trust? While this is an area that you will want to discuss with your attorney and a financial professional, it is likely that any retirement accounts — IRAs, 403(b)s, 401(a)s, 401(k)s, or Roth IRAs — will not be titled to the trust, but to the beneficiaries. Retirement accounts are typically not distributed through legal documents but through beneficiary designations. Because these are "individual" retirement accounts and have provisions based on age — since we can't answer the question "When will your trust reach retirement age?" — then we know that titling these assets to a trust will negate their fundamental structure; putting these assets in the trust creates the potential for double taxation. Instead, retirement accounts can be paid outright to the beneficiaries named on those accounts, avoiding the tax issues, if you wish.

Often, consumers create estate tax problems when they put the trust as the beneficiary of an IRA. You not only run the risk of double taxation, but the proceeds would have to be immediately paid out to the heirs, who can't then stretch the IRA across their life expectancy and create greater wealth for themselves. Perhaps you do want those IRAs to go through the trust, but you may want to discuss this with your attorney to see if you would benefit from structuring the trust with an IRA provision in it, the details of which are complicated and beyond the scope of this discussion but which you can discuss with your estate planning attorney.

Again, it's important to assess and review your legal documents with your attorney on an annual basis, because things may change in your family, or change with your beneficiaries, your heirs, or your property. If your documents don't reflect those changes, they won't work as efficiently as they should. There could be a situation in which you had a trust, but because of some unforeseen legal ramifications you might need to revoke that trust and create a new legal document to protect yourself. So don't take lightly the need to become educated on the proper legal documents to best represent your wishes.

One thing we can guarantee you as you consider your estate planning needs: life happens, things change in the lives of our loved ones, and laws change. So don't go at it alone and make sure as you think about estate planning, you create with the help of the estate planning professionals, a customized estate plan that integrates all components of your financial life.

CHAPTER THREE

Keeping What You've Got and Growing It

"Our goals can only be achieved through a vehicle of a plan in which we must fervently believe and upon which we must vigorously act. There is no other route to success."
– Pablo Picasso

A s a retirement and lifetime income professional, I've seen too many women suffer because of ill-informed decisions about their money and estate planning.

Sometimes disasters happen just because of a lack of decision making. Let's talk a little about financial literacy, because we want women to become wiser when it comes to their need to plan for their retirement years, the second and third phases of their lives, to ensure that they protect and preserve the quality of their lifestyles. That's what it's all about. At the end of the day, it's not a function of how much you have; it's a function of how much you keep that affords you the lifestyle you want for yourself and for those you love, whether they are your children, brothers, sisters, friends, etc.

One of the most important ways to help ensure this is to become financially literate so you can hold onto what you have accumulated, and properly understand the difference between investing and saving. The differences in these two disciplines and approaches to retirement income strategies could fill a book — in fact, that is the focal point of one of my books, "Retirement Done Right: Don't Just Invest ... Plan!" But to boil it down, let's go over key points for us as women to embrace in the area of basic financial principles. Remember, ladies, financial literacy has nothing to do with our aptitude or abilities. Many of us were simply not taught as young girls when we were growing up to assume financial management responsibilities. As I mentioned earlier, that lack of knowledge is typical of what we see with many baby boomer women. It's not that we are not intelligent enough for it, or that we don't have the capability; it's simply that we weren't taught to do it or perhaps had no female role models to follow. Just to be clear, I am speaking as a boomer woman who was raised with the attitude that "a man was my plan," and that I didn't need to worry about financial matters, let alone financial concepts and investing principles. I learned the hard way when I woke up one day and realized I was a caregiver for myself, two family members, and had to figure out how to manage and invest my savings to protect not only my family, but myself well into the future.

In order to become good stewards of our money, we have to understand various savings strategies and available options, and the risks and rewards associated with those strategies. We need to learn to understand and embrace investment risk in spite of our general tendency toward safety and security.

In the previous chapter, we talked about legal documents that protect our assets. Now we have to create a plan to help ensure we won't run out of money, which seems to be a prevailing fear of the boomer population. We have to develop good money management practices. We have to learn the basics of IRAs and pension plans, because at the end of the day, we need to know how to min-imize the most critical risks to our retirement years, including the risk of outliving our savings. We need to understand how to di-versify our investments wisely. Financial literacy helps us make a proper lifetime income plan to help ensure our savings will be there for us when we need it — even if live beyond 100.

The risk of inflation is another major challenge to planning for a secure future. We have to allow for the probability that our dol-lars will buy less down the road. Another hazard we need to ad-dress is how quickly we are going to spend down our savings. I call it creating a financial red zone (or, more simply stated, the "moment of truth") — it's that timeframe when you run out of money. How quickly are you going to get to that red zone? That red zone says I could wake up one morning and I might be 72 years old (a typical age at which I see many women run out of money), my savings spent, and I am going to end up living on So-cial Security. That's why I call it the moment-of-truth reality. Avoiding that trap requires that we anticipate this risk, so we can plan well in order to eliminate it. Proper planning is key to erasing the red zone and living a life of confidence and empowerment.

One of the more important considerations is saving enough money to cover the ever-increasing cost of health care (both rou-tine medical and preventative care and skilled nursing care), par-ticularly important for women because we have greater longevity. The good news is that we probably are going to live very long lives, perhaps into our early hundreds. The bad news is also that some of us may live into our hundreds, because as we age, women tend to experience more debilitating health care conditions and situations that start nipping away at our assets.

So how do you start? How do we become wise women in re-gard to ensuring we have the quality of the lifestyles we have worked for and have earned throughout our lifetime?

First, we have to start learning about investing. We have to start learning how to save first, and then invest those savings. We have to start differentiating between saving and investing. Generally speaking, a woman's retirement income strategy should be diversified and allow for opportunities for investments to beat the rising costs of the goods and services that we need (that's called inflation!), because if we don't do that, our money is going to lose purchasing power, and that loss of purchasing power with the increasing longevity that we are experiencing will not keep pace with inflation. Then we will have created a red zone for ourselves, and are likely to outlive our assets.

When we get a financial statement, we need to understand how to read and interpret it. Financial statements are not intended to be filed away or crammed in a drawer without looking at them. Far too often, my female clients tell me they don't even open the envelopes in which their financial statements come. Keeping our heads in the sand about where we stand magnifies the risk of ending up in the red zone.

Another way to help you keep what you have is to do the proper tax planning. And when I say "proper tax planning," I mean that we are living in a reality as a baby boomer generation in which the majority of the assets we've accumulated while working will probably be in tax-deferred accounts. These are various types of retirement accounts on which we did not pay the taxes while we were working. We got tax benefits by contributing to these retirement accounts. But when we start using the money during our retirement, it's going to be taxed as ordinary income. Let's say I have been saving 10 percent of my income every year over the last 30 years, and now I walk away with $300,000 in what is called a 401(k), or a 403(b), 401(a), deferred compensation plan, traditional IRA, simple IRA, or any of the familiar tax-deferred accounts. I may assume that I have $300,000 saved for retirement, but I really don't have that much, because none of it has been taxed. The thought process during our accumulation years (the years we are saving for retirement) is that we are saving in tax-deferred accounts so that, when we retire and use these assets, we will be in a lower tax bracket, and thus we will use this money in a tax-efficient manner. During retirement, we expect to pay fewer taxes on the money we saved for our retirement, but guess what? Taxes have increased and might continue to increase, thus impacting the lifestyle that we have worked so hard to create. In fact, we're living in an uncertain tax environment. I don't know about you, but I'm a boomer woman, and when I was saving in my 401(k), I never realized my Medicare premium was going to be based on my income, which includes the distributions I take out of my IRAs. Nor did I realize that up to 85 percent of my Social Security benefit could be taxed, again based on the distributions I take from my IRAs or other tax-deferred accounts. So, like many of you, we didn't know the rules of the retirement journey game, and now we need definitive plans to figure it out and keep more of the money we've saved or are eligible for in our pockets.

Theoretically, it is a good concept. Practically, in my opinion, it is a lousy concept, and it is tripping us all up today. By some estimates, the baby boomers will pay more than $2 trillion in taxes over the next decades because of these tax-deferred accounts that are, in effect, an "IOU to the IRS," and that's all they are.[19] Just remember, even though you may not be paying taxes on these accounts now, you will have to pay taxes on them later when you start taking your money out of these financial accounts, regardless of where you have positioned the funds.

The bottom line on these tax-deferred accounts is that they require us to do solid tax planning in advance to minimize our tax

---

[19] Dan Kadlec. Time, Money. June 27, 2016. "Why a $2 Trillion Tax Bill is Coming Due for Baby Boomers." http://time.com/money/4377233/retirement-boomers-taxes-required-withdrawals/. Accessed March 16, 2017.

liability. There are good ways in which to use our tax-deferred accounts, and there are not-so-good ways of using these accounts. Working with qualified tax advisors who are working directly with our financial advisors (the two professional disciplines are not the same) to create effective and efficient tax strategies will allow us the opportunity to minimize our tax burdens as we use the money during retirement, and also if we leave it as inheritances for our beneficiaries. The right tax plans and strategies can allow us to distribute those particular retirement account to our heirs with minimal tax obligations, as well.

Studies have shown that people who become educated about their financial strategies and play an active role in planning and monitoring their assets end up twice as wealthy as those who haven't a clue about how those accounts are going to be used.[20] So how do you protect the assets you spent a lifetime building from excessive taxation? Ed Slott, America's IRA expert and "best source of IRA advice," as acclaimed by The Wall Street Journal, offers some great guidance. Here are his five easy steps to protect your retirement resources.

The *first* is timing the use of your IRAs very smartly. For instance, if you use them before you're 59 ½, there's a 10 percent penalty, which means you lose that 10 percent of your assets. Also, the government requires that, whether you need them or not, you have to start taking payments from IRAs when you hit age 70 ½. You'll pay a 50 percent penalty to the IRS if you don't take what is called that required minimum distribution every year based on the value of your IRA. Believe me, this is serious: I recently had a client come in who had a small IRA and had not taken the required

---

[20] Annamaria Lusardi, Pierre-Carl Michaud, Olivia S. Mitchell. Oct. 9, 2014. Global Financial Literacy Excellence Center Working Paper. "Optimal Financial Knowledge and Wealth Inequality." https://papers.ssrn.com/sol3/papers2.cfm?abstract_id=2585222. Accessed March 1, 2017.

distributions for more than 18 years. Yes, he gets to pay a 50 percent penalty on the amount he should have withdrawn, and that is not the situation you want to find yourself in. Also, should you be in the fortunate group of boomers who don't need to take distributions out of their tax-deferred accounts, there are ways in the tax code, qualified charitable distributions, or QCDs, that allow you to contribute up to $100,000 annually of your IRA to a qualified charity and not pay the taxes. But, this needs to be assessed for appropriateness based on your lifetime income plan and the needs of your spouse/partner or other beneficiaries. There is no easy answer; it takes customized planning!

The *second* way to protect your retirement savings is to insure them. The combination of estate taxes and income taxes can consume a significant portion of your estate, so a good defense for protecting your retirement account might be life insurance, because life insurance is income-tax free to your beneficiaries and to your estate. If you have life insurance, you can keep the life insurance out of your estate by putting it in a gift trust or having someone other than yourself own it.

The *third* way is to stretch the IRA to your heirs. What is a stretch IRA? A stretch IRA is also known as a multigenerational IRA or a legacy IRA. It's not a product, so don't go looking for that. It's a process of how to stretch the value of that IRA, not only over your heirs' lifespans, but even over multiple generations, perhaps to children and grandchildren. To stretch it simply means you keep your inherited IRA account growing tax-deferred for your beneficiary for as long as is legally possible. It is one way to help build your family's wealth. Let's face it: many of the children of the baby boomers have not been the savers their parents' generation was, and don't have any (or sufficient) retirement savings themselves, so this is one way of giving your heirs an effective plan for retirement income.

The *fourth* strategy to protect your retirement savings is to consider a Roth conversion. What is a Roth IRA? It is an IRA that is taxed on the front end; since you pay your taxes upfront, you can then put your after-tax dollars into a Roth IRA that will grow tax free, can be used tax free, and does not require that minimum distributions be taken out. Of course, this is a simplified description of Roth IRAs, as they, too, have restrictions, as well as required distributions, should a non-spouse inherit one. A Roth conversion is a process whereby you take your existing IRA — your 401(k), 403(b), traditional IRA, or simple IRA — and convert it to a Roth. This means you pay taxes on 100 percent of that conversion in the tax year in which you converted these funds, but now you're able to grow that Roth IRA tax-free. You can use it tax-free once the Roth account has been open for five years or if you are 59 ½, or your children can inherit it as a tax-free asset. Roth conversions are not "one size fits all." It takes extensive planning and analysis to determine whether Roth conversions are appropriate, because you must consider how the taxes are going to be paid; you have to consider what your life expectancy is, what tax structure you're in now versus a tax structure we anticipate in the future, and many other considerations. There are those who say that everybody should do a Roth conversion, but that is not prudent advice at all. It requires tax planning and lifetime income planning, as well as estate planning, to determine the best way to leave that legacy to your loved ones. As a general rule, if you are going to use your IRA assets during the early stages of your retirement, it rarely makes sense to do a conversion.

The *fifth* and last way to protect your retirement savings that I will mention here is to avoid the death tax trap: estate taxes. Of course, the best way to avoid the death tax is to live forever, but because we know we're not going to live forever, we want to make sure that we have the appropriate legal documents to help protect us from estate taxes, which we talked about earlier in the book. The proper legal documents can keep that killer 50 to 60 percent of your estate from going to taxes. As I mentioned earlier, it is important that your trust is not the beneficiary of your IRAs, because if your trust receives the IRA you could potentially get into a double taxation situation. And none of us want that!

Now I'd like to move to addressing seven common mistakes retirees make with their finances. More than 40 percent of retirees report that their No. 1 biggest fear is that they're going to outlive their assets.[21] Your best defense against that is planning. A nationally known Certified Financial Planner by the name of Mike Reese identified the seven financial mistakes that retirees make. Make sure they don't apply to you!

The *first* and foremost is investing as though you're still working, because retirement represents a fundamental change in your life, and your portfolio should fundamentally shift as well. The allocations you use to accumulate wealth are often inappropriate when you're in a phase where you have to start utilizing or distributing those assets, so it's important to consider that your investment strategies may need to change throughout the various stages of your life. Investing is oriented around your life stage, so you should revisit your strategies as you navigate through the various life stages.

The *second* financial mistake is not protecting yourself and your retirement assets and nest egg from significant market drops. Here you can apply the prudent investor's Rule of 100 to get an idea of where you stand. Start with the number 100; then subtract your age. What is left is the percentage of your money that you might consider positioning in risk-based investments. Let me give you

---

[21] Transamerica Center for Retirement Studies. December 2016. "17th Annual Transamerica Retirement Survey." https://www.transamericacenter.org/docs/default-source/retirement-survey-of-workers/tcrs2016_sr_retirement_survey_of_workers_compendium.pdf. Accessed March 16, 2017.

an example. If I am 60 years old and we start with the base of 100, I subtract 60 from 100, and I end up with 40. According to this rule, I should have no more than 40 percent of my assets at risk. The other 60 percent should be put into fixed and guaranteed products and solutions. Even though they may not keep up with inflation, we need protection against market volatility when we are drawing on our savings to pay for our lifestyles. Now, of course this is only a guideline, a non-absolute starting point for assessing your own risk tolerance.

Yet, even judging by this baseline, based on what I see in my own practice, most women are taking significantly more financial risk than they should be taking. I believe women can preserve the integrity of their lifestyles and the ability to do the things that they want to do for themselves and their loved ones by taking far less risk than they are typically taking. Losing a significant amount in your portfolio is a major threat to the quality of your retirement; add the longevity risk factor and we have some major hurdles that could create significant issues. When it comes to your retirement income, a portion of that income should be guaranteed — regardless of what is happening in the market, regardless of what's happening in the economy, regardless of what interest rates are. You need guarantees for basic lifestyle expenses!

That brings me to the **third** financial mistake, which is not guaranteeing basic income needs. What do I mean by that? There is a retirement lifestyle that we're trying to protect based on basic needs, or core lifestyle costs. Your guaranteed income sources should take into consideration those basic income needs: keeping the lights on, keeping the food coming in, keeping the gas in the car, keeping the car maintained, maintaining the house. It's very important to ensure that those expenses are financially covered, because they will always be there regardless of what goes on in our economy or with life events. Sadly, in my experience, when I ask the individual or family I'm working with how much they need to maintain their core lifestyle, there is usually silence. This is a high-risk road to retirement income planning. The most crucial data point you need to understand is how much you need for core lifestyle expenses.

The *fourth* financial mistake most retirees make is the cost of their assets that they have under management. It's one thing to lose the value of your retirement assets when the market goes down significantly, but it's another thing to lose the value of your assets due to the costs associated with various types of asset management fees, transaction costs, or mutual fund fees and charges. Let me give you an example: let's say that you had a mutual fund of $200,000 in your portfolio for 10 years, and the management fee in that mutual fund is 2 percent. If there's a 20 percent internal fund fee (2 percent for 10 years), that's $40,000 in fees over the 10 years you have held that mutual fund. Now if you have a 20 percent loss due to market volatility, that's an additional $40,000 loss. So you can see the magnitude of risks to the quality of your lifestyle. In my experience, most investors are not paying enough attention to expenses and fees in those portfolios that are being managed by their advisers. Growth of your assets is a function of market performance (plus or minus) and the fees. The fees are always there, whether you are making money or not! Any product or service has a price, and it is important to understand what that price is, and to see if you can reduce fees and costs to help your funds grow, uninhibited.

The *fifth* financial mistake is inadequate tax planning, and we touched on that earlier when we addressed IRAs. Most of us have a tax preparer. You may go to the local H&R Block or AARP tax services at a retail level. But really, the employees of these companies don't know anything about our financial situation; they just are tax preparers. This is one of the most common mistakes we make each year. It's important that we shift the mindset, getting away from a tax preparer and moving into getting ourselves a tax planner. Most accountants aren't tax planners. They're tax preparers. Some financial professionals do tax planning and some of them don't. It's prudent on our part to ensure that we have a tax planner, because as we start using more of those retirement accounts or retirement assets, we start paying more taxes. And yes, Social Security benefits could potentially be taxed! Imagine that, a tax in addition to a tax that we paid while we were working. There are so many ways we can be blindsided by taxes that eat into the money we've saved or are entitled to, whether it's our IRAs or our Social Security income. A tax planner can help you come up with a way to minimize that bite; a tax preparer can't. One of my strategic partners in my firm, a prominent CPA, says it best about his services and the value of sound tax advice: "We're an investment, not an expense." This is how we should value good tax planning advice: as an investment in our financial security and not as an expense where we desire to cut costs. Be thoughtful about taxes embedded in the income/growth of your investments. There are differences between tax treatment of mutual funds and exchange-traded funds. Rarely does a CPA identify the fact that your financial advisor may be creating a situation of increased taxes. It's best to get all of your financial professionals to talk to each other about your goals and how you can hold on to more of your financial assets through proper, integrated planning.

The *sixth* financial mistake is thinking that your traditional IRA is always a good thing, which we discussed earlier. IRAs can be a perpetual tax liability throughout your retirement years. I can't stress enough how important proper IRA distribution planning is with regard to tax planning.

Some of those unexpected life events — divorce or widowhood — can also have a massive effect on your taxes. When we're married, we file jointly; those tax tables are more favorable than filing single. All of a sudden, a widow can see her income go down after the death of her husband *and* have her tax bill go up. I'll never forget the day I visited with a recently widowed client, right after the first tax period since her husband's passing. She called me in hysterics because she had never had to pay taxes and now had a big tax bill. She thought she was doing something wrong, because she had a $5,500 tax bill, but when we looked at it, we saw it was a function of filing as single rather than married filing jointly. It was a nasty surprise, and we don't want those surprises, so planning for tax implications of major life events in advance is very important.

The *seventh* financial mistake most retirees make is not knowing how much liquidity they need in retirement. Most of us don't want to ever touch our principal as we move into retirement, and we see all the models that say, "If you have enough money you just take 4 percent out every year and you live on that." Well, what if you can't generate 4 percent? The message here is that it's not all or none. You need to protect your nest egg and make sure you have liquidity while living off of the income that your nest egg generates. There are different ways of generating income guarantees that may not offer immediate liquidity. Essentially, you need your money to possess three attributes during your retirement journey: safety, liquidity, and growth. The bad news is that you can't have all three in one financial tool; the good news is that a financial life plan can provide all three. You simply need a plan that balances guaranteed sources of income with your need for liquidity for emergency situations that will arise during retirement. When you're looking at investments, it's important to look at the growth potential of the principal, along with your need to maintain liquidity, which is the ability to access the money whenever you need it without penalty. Those two goals could potentially conflict, which requires us to do significant planning. If you put the money in a six-month CD that might pay you only 1 ½ percent, you're losing purchasing power, and that's a risk to your growth potential. There is a tradeoff here that must be considered.

Another hazard that can impact your ability to hold on to your assets pertains to second or third marriages. Blended families are a new norm with their own potential financial pitfalls. Your kids, his kids, our kids, your future — there are a lot of things to consider. I have seen situations in second marriages in which the spouse passes away without proper legal documents, the widow discovers that his children from a previous marriage receive 50 percent of all assets in the estate, and the grieving wife is left with substantially less than what she had anticipated, and in some cases without a home. Don't let that happen to you. Make sure that if you are contemplating a second marriage and there are children from each previous marriage, you have the money conversation *before* the ceremony. Afterward is often too late. You and your prospective spouse may have very different ideas about what to do with your respective and blended estates. Don't set yourself up for an unpleasant surprise. Get clear on that ahead of the need.

An important tool in helping you to protect your assets is making sure you have the proper insurance. Wise women protect themselves from the risk of financial loss in many different ways. For example, we have homeowners' insurance that protects our finances from fire, from catastrophe, from hurricanes, and from floods. We have disability insurance as we are working that typically protects our income if we become disabled, so that we can continue getting our checks. We have life insurance that will protect us against an income loss in the event that the spouse or partner who is the primary breadwinner unexpectedly dies. We have health insurance that protects us from debilitating costs of health care in the event of a catastrophic illness or injury. Many of us have vision and dental insurance that will help us defray some of the costs of those kinds of care, or insurance that covers the costs of prescription drugs. We also often protect ourselves with long-term-care insurance (and this is an essential consideration for all women over 60, since seven out of 10 individuals will most likely need some form of skilled nursing care!).[22]

In the same way that we use insurance to protect us from financial loss in these other areas, one area where you can protect yourself is in insurance for income, to help ensure that you never run out of money. That is a good way to keep what you have, and is probably more important than some of these other kinds of insurance, again because women have a much longer life expectancy, and that means retirement is going to cost us more. It is important to make sure that living longer doesn't mean that we are going to live poorer or that we are going to run out of money. Many wise women include annuities among their financial strategies in the fixed-income portion of their savings so that it's not just stocks, bonds, CDs, and money market accounts, or other types of traditional assets.

So what's an annuity? I'm glad you asked, because it may be the most misunderstood financial tool in the financial industry.

An annuity can be simply defined as guaranteed income. Just like all the other types of insurance contracts, whether it's life, health, disability, or property and casualty insurance, it is a contract with an insurance company to provide you with a series of regular payments, either immediate or at a later time in your life. In exchange for purchasing the annuity with a single premium payment or multiple payments, the insurance company — backed by its own financial strength and claims-paying ability — guarantees that it will pay you income for the contract term, even if that is for the rest of your life and even your spouse's life.

For example, I give the insurance company $100,000 to put into an annuity for me. They can either start paying me back with

---

[22] LongTermCare.gov. "The Basics." https://longtermcare.acl.gov/the-basics/index.html. Accessed May 5, 2017.

that money immediately, or I can tell them to hold it for three or five years (or any other time frame I desire based on my planning and income needs) and then give me a series of monthly payments for the rest of my life. That is basically how we "insure for income," because this is the only financial tool that can be guaranteed to provide an income that you can't outlive. As I mentioned in an earlier chapter, we have a very real issue in that women often have fewer assets, fewer pension plans, and greater risks of needing long-term care because they are more likely to suffer debilitating illnesses.

Is an annuity right for you, and what type of annuity is best? An annuity is a solution to an income need that you anticipate, and choosing the right annuity is a function of a detailed plan. Adding an annuity to your retirement portfolio is not to be taken lightly; annuities are planning tools and cannot be sold without an appropriate plan, although that is how most consumers acquire them — through sales agents of insurance companies or brokerage firms that use a "one-size-fits-all" model. The choice depends on your particular circumstances: your income needs, whether you have other types of protection for long-term care, and various other considerations of that nature. It requires careful planning, and when it comes to income protection, one size does not fit all.

There are four basic types of annuities, some of which could be very good and others very bad for you, depending on your situation, particularly if they are acquired without having a detailed plan. A variable annuity is essentially another type of an investment account. It's something you'd be more likely to find in a professionally managed portfolio, depending on your investment objectives, tolerance for risk, and the time horizon you have before needing to use these assets. As the name implies, it is variable, which means, for instance, that if I purchase a variable annuity with $100,000, it could grow 5 percent, 10 percent, 15 percent, or more. It could also decrease by 5 percent, 10 percent, 15 percent, etc. Its gain or loss is based on market performance. With the variable annuity, you can get optional riders to guarantee the original principle, or perhaps a death benefit, or minimum income values. In addition to market volatility, the performance of variable annuities may be heavily impacted and influenced by fees. But variable annuities are predominantly investment vehicles typically found in an investment portfolio. Typically, when someone gets to be about 50 years old and has a short horizon for use of the asset, a variable annuity may not be a proper solution, because it is too risk-based and you can't control the risk in it. It's a function of the funds that are contained in that management portfolio. But if you're 35 or 40, it's potentially a very useful tool. Again, it needs to be directly linked to a broader plan.

A second type of annuity is an immediate annuity. An immediate annuity is just that: immediate. You give an insurance company a lump sum of money, say $100,000, for a contractual guarantee of income. In return for that you are guaranteed to receive predictable, regular payments that begin immediately. An advantage of this type of annuity is that it will pay you for life, regardless of how long you live. The disadvantage is that it will pay you *only* for life, regardless of how long you live. So if you live only two years into the contract, it's gone. If you gave money to the company for the contract on the promise that it would guarantee you income for life, that means *your* life. If you live to 120, the company will pay you that income to age 120. But when you die, whenever you die, the balance is the company's. You can also choose a payout option that gives you income for a minimum period of time ("period certain") or for a "period certain or life" option. The company will reduce the payment that it gives you, because it will be required to pay for a minimum of the period certain or life, whichever comes first. If I opt for payout for five years and I die in two years, the company is still going to pay my beneficiary for the three years following my death. If I live past five years, it will pay me for life.

While an immediate annuity is a reliable source of income, it doesn't offer you growth, and it doesn't offer any other features. First and foremost, it is simply an immediate guarantee that you are going to get income. This is a proper choice for certain life situations, but not for everyone, so it's key that you know whether it is appropriate for you. Again, remember that appropriateness of any financial solution is a function of a well-defined and clearly articulated lifetime income plan.

The next type is called a fixed annuity. With a fixed annuity, an insurance company provides you with a guaranteed interest rate for a specific number of years, and helps protect your money from market fluctuation. While the contract does not have an "end date," the interest rates credited are typically guaranteed for a set period of time, after which they will be re-established based on current market conditions. For example, let's say I purchase a fixed annuity with a $100,000 premium and the company's current interest rate guarantee is 3 percent for five years. I am guaranteed that rate (subject to the company's strength and claims-paying ability) for those five years. At the end of those five years, the company can set a new interest rate for another guaranteed time period. Or, I could decide to surrender my annuity after the first five years if I don't want to lock in at the new interest rate.

There are different ways to access your money in this annuity. You can turn on lifetime income, you can convert it to an immediate annuity, or you can continue the annuity at the new interest rate to continue the tax-deferral benefits. Annuities themselves are tax-deferred, allowing you to defer taxes on interest earned until the funds are withdrawn. Keep in mind that putting an annuity into an IRA or other qualified plan does not offer any additional tax benefits though — both an IRA and an annuity offer tax deferral, so if you are considering purchasing the annuity within your IRA, you will want to ensure that you are doing this for reasons other than tax deferral, such as the guaranteed income stream and lifetime benefits.

Additionally, in most cases, annuities are protected from creditor claims or claims arising from lawsuits. Covering all possibilities here is beyond the scope of this book, but the key to this type of annuity is the guaranteed interest rate that is fixed and won't change for the duration of whatever the contractually guaranteed interest rate period is.

A more recent type of annuity is called the fixed index annuity. Whereas the variable annuity can go up and down with the market, the fixed index annuity earns interest tied to the market, but it is a fixed insurance product and is guaranteed not to lose money due to market drops, because your money is never actually invested in the market. The annuity offers a guaranteed interest rate — often it's as low as 0-1 percent — but this ensures that you don't lose money due to market losses. You then get the opportunity to earn interest based on select market indexes, although that interest is limited each year by factors like a cap, spread or participation rate. This gives you the potential to earn interest that is greater than you may get with a fixed annuity. Also, with the fixed index annuity, you have the opportunity to add an optional lifetime income rider for a fee that will provide you with a higher income payout than the annuity can alone. As with other types of annuities, you can create income for you and often for your spouse that neither of you will ever outlive.

Now, let's change our focus and talk a little about financial management — about making an important shift in how we think about money. Something specific to women is that we tend to be spenders more than investors. Whether we're spending on ourselves or on our children or grandchildren, we tend to be spenders. Women have a heart for their family, always spending on family first, not realizing that someday we will be in need of a lot of money to protect our senior years.

I invite women to shift that spending mindset into more of a saving/investing mindset, because we are going to have to save more money than we habitually do now. Our longevity and the rising costs of health care, along with the fact that our income is not going to keep up with those costs, necessitate that we focus on saving/ investing through the various stages of our lives and well into our senior (or more mature) years.

That's why I think women should adopt more prudent money management practices. I have many women tell me, "You know, I can barely keep up with my bills every month. How do you expect me to save when I can't even make ends meet?"

My typical response is, "Well, let's forget that for now." Here is a simple strategy that I encourage women to embrace, and it's one that helped me save over 15 percent more during my working years. What I would like you to do is get a little journal and keep track of your spending for 30 days. Make sure your journal is small enough to fit into your purse so you've always got it with you, and write down every little thing you spend your money on. I don't care if you spend a dollar for a pack of chewing gum or stop and get a soda for $1.25. Write down *everything* you spend for 30 days.

At the end of that 30 days, sit down with your journal, categorize your spending into themes, review what you spent, and look to see what is essential and what isn't. I guarantee you, ladies, when that is done, you will typically find $200 to $350 that could be shifted to savings or more contributions toward a 401(k) or to other types of investment vehicles. I encourage every woman to do this cash-flow analysis, because you'll be surprised at how easy it is to save once you realize where you're "leaking" cash. We have very simple, user-friendly tools on our website available to you when you work with our Woman's Worth® team of professionals, and I hope you'll take a moment and try them, because it's all about your long-term financial security. From your cash-flow analysis, you can begin to create a budget sheet (there's a sample sheet in the back of this book for you). Once you create a budget, stick to it. There is power in your pocketbook when you're working with a budget and when you feel good about sticking to it. You are financially empowering yourself, and the sky is the limit. A budget empowers you to make more sound choices and decisions.

Here are some nuggets of wisdom that I want to leave you with to help facilitate your journey toward financial empowerment. These are tips only, and may not all apply to you, but they have worked very well for me and many of the women I serve in helping create financial life plans:

- Consider how many credit cards you have. Having many, or more than two, really, could be a financial no-no. Especially if any have high interest rates or annual fees, think about reducing the number of cards you carry and keep the ones with the lowest rates and fees.
- Pay off your credit card bills and any high-interest loans. Go after them aggressively and pay them down.
- If you can't afford something, don't charge it.
- Always comparison shop before you buy.
- Save for something and then buy it after you have saved the cash to pay for it. You get an unbelievable psychological reward when you can just go and buy something with cash and not charge it.
- Make sure that a fixed percentage of your income is always deposited directly into savings, where you don't even see it, touch it, or feel it. This is called "Paying Yourself First."
- Accelerate the growth of your nest egg by taking all that money that you save by using coupons at the grocery store or elsewhere, and put 100 percent of what you save into a special account. These days the grocery store prints what

you've saved on your receipt every time you spend money. If your receipt says you saved $12.45, put that $12.45 into that savings account. Do the same at the department stores where they give you a receipt for your new clothes you purchased on sale and with an "additional 30% off" bargain. Truly get in the mindset that you "saved" that money for your future. You will not believe what it will do for your financial future.

- Break a habit. Stop smoking, stop drinking 5 or 6 sodas a day, quit buying lottery tickets; no more "I can't pass up a bargain." Break the habit and shift that money you would have spent into an investment vehicle.
- Stop spending money on your adult children or excessive money on your grandchildren. Sometimes exercising a bit of "tough love" in and of itself could protect your financial future.
- Most important, don't loan money to family or friends if you can't afford to lose the funds, because you may not get the money back. Just don't do that.

There is a series of hazards and mistakes that women need to avoid in getting involved in managing the family's finances. What we find in working with most couples is that the women go ahead and manage the operational budget, just handling the day-to-day stuff: keeping the house maintained, meeting the basic family needs, and keeping the kids functioning. But women typically don't get involved in the more strategic investment plans and choices, and they need to avoid this critical mistake. Wise women get involved in financial planning for the long term by getting actively and proactively involved in avoiding debt. We need to stop spending money we don't have on kids and grandkids. If you aren't thinking strategically, you will just keep spending on the kids and grandkids, and this is where you have to exercise tough love. Remember, ladies, you will most likely outlive your spouse or partner by an average of nine years! Ask yourself, "Do I want to live poor in my elder years, or do I want to live in prosperity?"

And for those of you who are in relationships and co-mingle all of your financial assets, let's face it, we as women spend more on our kids, on our clothes, and so on. But you may also be in a relationship where a lot of the funds are going toward recreational "toys," not just on routine spending. I know I'm meddling now, but way too often I see couples' resources spent on very expensive toys such as boats, motorcycles, sports vehicles, antique car parts, etc. Could those resources be better used in your retirement income strategy? I invite you to validate whether these types of expenses protect your financial future, or put you at risk.

Another pitfall is that we tend to spend our tax returns. Women need to stop spending the tax return when it comes back. First of all, we have already lost interest because we loaned our money to the government; when we get it back, wise women reinvest it to recover the interest earnings we lost while the IRS held our hard-earned money. We need to face the fact that we will likely end up living on our own someday, possibly with less income and just one primary source of income, so we need a healthy nest egg. Another pitfall is that women tend to procrastinate about having proper legal documents that can protect them and their heirs (as discussed in the previous chapter). And, as important, women often do not get professional guidance about finances soon enough because they are "too embarrassed" to talk to others about where they are financially and disclose their fears, concerns, or realities.

One of the more important trends that we are seeing in the working generation is the value they put on young mothers choosing to stay at home and pursue their caregiving roles with their young children. Homeschooling is on the rise, and this is a nonpaid profession, so the opportunity to save in employer-sponsored retirement accounts is nonexistent. In these circumstances, often the majority of the retirement assets are accumulated by the husband, which is a concern. Women need to do their own preparation for retirement, which could mean opening a spousal IRA, in which both spouses can contribute regularly, or it could mean opening other investments to help accumulate funds for the spouse at home. After all, the women are working in a nonpaying caregiving role for the benefit of the family, and retirement assets should be accumulated as a reward for their commitment to this role. Ladies, please insist on a savings plan for yourself, and get involved in managing your money to develop your skills in asset management on a smaller scale before you are thrown into the fire to manage a much larger asset mix and portfolio.

All of this suggests that, as we look to protect and preserve the lifestyle we desire for our future, we have to do the proper integrated life planning, financial management, retirement income planning, and analysis; we have to have sound tax planning and asset management; and we have to create and maintain a life plan that is flexible, easy to understand, and reviewed annually, at a minimum. All of these considerations are essential components of a proper lifetime income plan, and as we have said before, if you fail to plan, you plan to fail!

CHAPTER FOUR

Creating a Lifetime Income Plan

"Self-discipline is the ability to make yourself do something you don't necessarily want to do, to get a result you would really like to have."
– Andy Andrews

When it comes to enjoying our lives in our more mature years, it's all about having the quality of lifestyle we desire. And the question for us is, do we want a guarantee and a certainty that we can protect and preserve the quality of our lifestyle, or do we want to be on a roller-coaster ride as we journey through our life stages due to unplanned life events, market volatility, unanticipated health care expenses, taxes we can't control, or a host of other "unknowns"?

There are other good reasons to have a solid lifetime income plan in place before you can begin thinking about retirement. Life-changing events occur spontaneously. A woman could find herself a 52-year-old widow; remember from earlier discussions, the average age of widowhood is 56. She could find herself in an unexpected divorce after a 25- or 30-year marriage. Also, no job is absolutely secure, so we have to be prepared. What will happen to us if we've planned on working until we are 65, only to find ourselves suddenly downsized in our 50s or 60s? Additionally, we have to create plans in the event we end up with a debilitating illness. Because we typically end up with fewer assets and live longer, lifetime income planning is important for women over the age of 40, and essential for women over 50. Do you have a life plan? And how do you create a life plan that protects your lifestyle, ensures financial well-being, and accommodates the unknown? Hang on; the journey is about to begin, and it is a journey that provides the foundation for total well-being, because, ladies, *it's more than the money; it's about total well-being!*

The first step is to create a lifestyle scenario. That lifestyle scenario will lead us to creating a life plan. Then we determine how much money and income we need to achieve the plan. We can start with the assessment of our sources of lifetime income, which typically come from three areas, and if there is any gap in those three areas, we have to create a plan to eliminate the gaps with certainty and predictability.

Social Security benefits are designed to replace approximately 40 percent of your income to support your lifestyle. The rest of your income in retirement must come from pensions — which many of us no longer have — and personal savings or investments. Many women try to live on a simple pension plan, but those pensions often come from employment in jobs that are traditionally lower-paying jobs, like the education or nursing professions, so they tend to be lower-than-average pensions. Some hope to live on Social Security, but nobody can live on Social Security alone. It is, at best, at the poverty level, which is why women are 80 percent more likely to be poor in their later years.[23]

---

[23] National Institute on Retirement Security. March 1, 2016. "Women 80% More Likely to be Impoverished in Retirement." http://www.nirsonline.org/index.php?option=content&task=view&id=913. Accessed Feb. 28, 2017.

Unfortunately, most women have negatively impacted their Social Security (by no fault of their own!), because, on the average, they have stepped out of the workforce for more than a decade to take on caregiving roles for their children, an aging relative, a parent, or a spouse. They've lost more than $300,000 in real-time earnings, plus more in benefits and compound interest from retirement savings accounts and employer matches.[24] Because of that, women tend to experience a significant negative impact to their pension plans and their Social Security calculations. Personal savings and investments become very, very critical for women as supplements to those two sources of income, so lifetime income planning is one of the most essential things we as women can do to protect our futures and keep ourselves from becoming part of and contributing to the elderly poor statistics.

I'll give you an example of some of the things that should be considered as you navigate the road to developing a life plan. If I am a golfer, and I want to play golf two times a week during my retirement with the league I am associated with, there are costs associated with that goal, such as cart fees, course fees, perhaps club membership dues, etc. I will need to build these factors into my personal scenario of the quality of life that I want in the future, and then apply dollars and cents to that vision of my future life to account for those expenses.

"Decisions determine your destiny!" How many of us may have heard this but never stopped to ponder what decisions will truly determine our destiny? As an entrepreneurial woman myself, and being in the baby boomer generation, I was never taught that the decisions I made throughout my lifetime could have a substantial impact on my financial security, including my retirement. I made

---

[24] Family Caregiver Alliance. February 2015. "Who Are the Caregivers?" https://www.caregiver.org/women-and-caregiving-facts-and-figures. Accessed Feb. 28, 2017.

short-term decisions, as many of us do, but didn't focus much attention on the major decisions that impact our destiny for the longer term. Decisions such as choosing a career, getting married, getting divorced, buying a home, having children, and saving and investing all impact the quality of the various stages of our retirement years. So why is it that we spend more time planning a dinner party, a wedding, a vacation, or even an evening out than we spend planning for the various stages of our life to ensure we have security? Even more alarming is that we associate planning with investing, which is far from the truth and a total misconception.

Life planning necessitates a focus on understanding your legal, financial, emotional, and physical requirements. This is essential to ensuring a smooth journey toward a successful financial future. The first step in a life plan starts with a personal financial checkup. As wise women, we take great care in getting our annual physical as a preventive measure to remain physically healthy and perhaps derail anything that could potentially lead to poor physical health. But when was the last time you had a financial physical?

Here are some questions that are typically addressed in a financial physical:

- Have you considered what annual income you will need in retirement or how long you might live during this phase of life?
- What do you want to do in the next phase of your life, and how much money will you need to do that?
- Do you have the proper legal documents that protect you and your family from unexpected life events?
- Are you concerned about having enough income in 10 to 20 years to keep up with inflation?
- Are you concerned about having to change your lifestyle in later years due to loss of spouse and perhaps his or her Social Security income or even a pension income?

- Are you concerned about loss of principal due to stock market volatility?
- Are you concerned about not knowing a way to "crash-proof" your estate for you, your spouse, and generations to come?
- Are you concerned about the three taxes that can reduce your IRAs and other retirement accounts (estate, state, and federal income taxes)?
- Do you have your money in joint financial accounts with adult children who are at risk of divorce, may have creditor issues, or are parties to lawsuits, etc.?
- Are you concerned you're paying too much in income and Social Security taxes?
- Are you concerned about nursing home expenses financially devastating your or your spouse's assets? What about funding routine medical costs that could spiral during your retirement journey?
- Have you thought about how you will handle your savings once you retire and what support you might need?
- Do your assets have protection from lawsuits or any creditors' claims?
- Do you know how much you can allocate for "self-care" to help ensure total well-being?

These items represent some of the areas that are typically addressed when you think about your life plan. They simply provide the necessary background information about the present so you can develop a road map for the journey to get you to the future with predictable outcomes and minimal surprises. Surprises can be overcome more easily when we are in our 30s and early 40s, but if you find yourself in your mid-40s or older and can't answer these questions, the journey through the golden years could include unnecessary surprises and emotional stress, which could ultimately impact your physical well-being.

Let's talk about painting the picture of that desired lifestyle. Let yourself dream; let yourself really visualize your dreams and desires and say, "These are the things I never was able to do when I was raising kids or when I was a caregiver or when I was worried about saving money." Does the money you have support the quality of the lifestyle in your dreams?

Think about the place you call home. Where do you want to live? Are you going to move to a different part of the country? Are you going to move to a different state? Maybe you're currently living in a state that doesn't have a state income tax, but want to move to a state that does have state income tax; that's an expense you'll have to consider. If you're staying where you are, you'll need to consider the maintenance costs on your home. Your home may need a new roof at $15,000, or a new heating system. Or your home may need a facelift or renovation — critical when we're thinking about our retirement lifestyle.

Then we look at transportation: How much is transportation costing you now versus in the future? If you're half of a couple, are you going to continue to have two cars when you both retire, or are you going to have one car? Are you going to have more costs for airfare, because your children live far away and you'll want to see them frequently or pay to have grandchildren come and visit you?

What about food — are you going to eat out more? Are you going to entertain friends and family more? How much are you spending for those types of costs now, versus the future? One of the critical factors that are overlooked in many plans is food for those four-legged family members that you have in your household, like your cats and dogs — very important. I have clients whose passion is to rescue pets that need homes, and we had to build into their retirement plan an $850-a-month expense for pet food and pet care. These expenses for our "best friends" are frequently neglected.

Let's not forget to factor in clothing and personal care. Maybe we were accustomed to keeping our clothing updated for our jobs, but we don't need as much expensive clothing for retirement. Maybe the costs shift from clothing to more personal care and maintenance. Most critical are health and medical expenses. How much more money are we going to need for those Medicare gap policies, or for those long-term-care policies? If you retire at 60, perhaps, or 62, how will you be insured in that gap time between your employee insurance and your eligibility for Medicare? Also, will you be joining a health club to maintain your health? If we're going to be living longer, we obviously have to be proactive in ensuring that we're healthy, and we'll talk about that at length later on in the book. Entertainment costs also fit in. Will you spend more or less money and time on movies, books, theater, shopping? How much money are you going to be spending on your hobbies? Are you going to take up a hobby? And also consider those leisure activities, like golfing, fishing, hiking — will you have to join a club or other facility to pursue those interests?

Many of us dream of having our golden years filled with beautiful travel, so we need to consider the costs associated with domestic and international travel. How much will you want to spend for your family-oriented travel, such as holiday visits or major life events for your children and grandchildren, versus pleasure-oriented travel?

Another factor that impacts our lifestyle is taxes: property taxes, federal and state income taxes, and capital gains taxes if you start buying and selling property. It's important to build a scenario for your desired lifestyle in terms of where and how you will live, as well. Also, do you have any debt that requires repayment? It may be wise to pay off that debt before you go into retirement, if you're paying it back at an interest rate higher than your assets are earning. In addition to taxes, we must factor in an appropriate allowance for inflation for our desired lifestyle.

Where will you age? Do you want to "age in place," which means staying in your home and, if so, do you need to consider some renovations or changes that allow you to do that? When I made the decision to have my family members age in place, my plan had to account for $135,000 in construction costs to ensure a handicapped accessible room. I also needed to account for the costs associated with bringing care in my home for my aging family members.

These are the kinds of things that must be built into a lifetime income plan, and that plan also has to reflect our changing requirements as we age. In considering the needs and desires appropriate to different life phases, I like to break down those stages as being between 50 and 60, 60 and 70, 70 and 80, and then 80 and beyond. The answers to the questions in all these categories and the expenses associated with them are different at each of these different stages, and it's important to take that into consideration, because there are implications for protecting and preserving the quality of your lifestyle. It's ridiculous for us to think that the cost for health care when we're 50 to 60 will be the same as the cost of health care in our 70-plus years.

I know a woman's heart is always with her children and grandchildren, and in spite of all the advice I give women to stop giving away their retirement assets to their children and grandchildren, they're going to be doing that. That's just how women are made, and we need to honor that God-ordained design. So how much do we want to allocate for gifting to our children and grandchildren in some capacity? We can continue to honor this special nature so often specific to women, but we need to put constraints on it. Remember, our goal is not to end up as an elderly poor woman, but rather as a prosperous woman in mind, body, and spirit.

When we take all of these variables into consideration, we can create a baseline. We need to figure a rate of inflation into it, as well as the rate of return that you can get on your assets. Then we can quantify what our quality of lifestyle is going to look like from a cost perspective, and how much money we will need to preserve the integrity of that desired lifestyle across our life span. There are numerous tools available to you from the Woman's Worth® team of professional income planners that will facilitate this discovery journey to ensure you have thought through the variables specific to your personal needs. Another tool is in the appendix at the back of this book and will guide you along this process.

Placing a concrete value on the costs associated with your dreams and desires is what a guide can help you do, so don't go at this alone. There is power in two-way dialogue with professionals who specialize in this type of planning. Remember, this is about life planning, not just financial planning. Identifying and creating your dreams and goals (the qualitative lifestyle) along with the concrete dollars and cents needed (the quantitative needs of the lifestyle) is the most painful part of the lifestyle-protection planning process. But it's key to bringing clarity to how large or small the gaps are in your journey toward achieving your desired lifestyle. Putting numbers to it and projecting out through your late 90s to your early 100s tells us where we need to be (yes, ladies, one out of every four 65-year-olds will live into their 90s, so plan for it!).[25] Inevitably there will be many gaps that are identified by this process, which will need to be converted into an action plan or a series of solutions. It's never a "one size fits all," because no two people have the same desires and lifestyle requirements. But your personal action plan gives you a guide that provides you with a life

---

[25] Social Security Administration. "Calculators: Life Expectancy." https://www.ssa.gov/planners/lifeexpectancy.html. Accessed March 1, 2017.

plan that helps you move from point A to point B with greater confidence, with point B being your desired retirement lifestyle, and point A being where you are today at the beginning of your planning. It's critical that you have a guide and facilitator in the crafting of this plan, a like-minded lifetime income planner who's conversant with the disciplines that we've talked about previously: the tax discipline, the asset management discipline, the legal planning discipline, and the health care planning discipline, all of which are critical to creating that plan for you. Look at this guide as your financial physical generalist who will identify all the specialists who need to be on your team to help you achieve your plan.

Statistically, only something like 48 percent of men and women have sat down to figure out how much income they might need in retirement.[26] Now, that doesn't even mean they have a strategy to attain that income, and it doesn't tell us whether they are prepared for emergencies. It just tells us that less than half of American workers have even put the bare minimum into preparing for income in retirement. By knowing today that I might have a problem in 10 years or 15 years, I can keep that problem from rearing its ugly head, because I can implement actions to prevent it. That's why it's important for us to ensure that we create that plan, to preserve the dignity of our retirement, free of anxiety, frustration, and deprivation. It allows us not only to do what we want for ourselves, but to do what we want to do for and with our loved ones.

Sometimes, the financial professionals who helped you accumulate your assets and the financial professionals who help you

---

[26] Ruth Helman, Craig Copeland, Jack VanDerhei. Employee Benefit Research Institute. April 2015. "The 2015 Retirement Confidence Survey: Having a Retirement Savings Plan a Key Factor in Americans' Retirement Confidence." https://www.ebri.org/pdf/briefspdf/EBRI_IB_413_Apr15_RCS-2015.pdf. Accessed March 16, 2017.

plan to distribute them in your golden years are not same people. Lifetime income and distribution planning is a very different process from just accumulating assets, and requires a different set of skills, competencies, and strategies. Not all financial professionals are proficient in working with both phases of your life, so you need to make sure that you have a team of experts on your side who are like-minded and march to the beat of your financial drum — it's about integration of *your* life plan.

Your life plan is a living, breathing plan. Look at it as your next best friend. Once you have this plan developed, it's not a plan that you put on the shelf to collect dust. Think of it as a baseline plan. You get a baseline colonoscopy when you're age 50. You get a baseline mammogram when you're 50, too, along with those baseline bone-density tests. We get all our baseline tests, and then every year or two thereafter we have checkups to compare where we are relative to our baselines. We have our health physicals that ensure that we're not deviating from that baseline, and if there is a deviation, very quickly we can put in some proactive measures that help us make sure that we can stay healthy and whole.

Your lifestyle income plan is no different, and we call that process the annual financial physical. It assesses where you are today on a yearly basis against that baseline plan we put together. If one of the gaps is that you need to accelerate savings by a certain amount a month, then we're going to look at it every year thereafter and see how you're tracking. That financial physical is essential to assess where you are, not only in your finances, but also in terms of possible changes to your legal documents: those wills, trusts, powers of attorney. Did anything happen with your heirs? For instance, I had a client who told me she had to adopt a grandson in her retirement years because he was autistic and her daughter could not care for him. He was on government assistance because of his disability, and if she left him any of her estate, that would disrupt his government assistance. Her estate planning attorney and I collaborated to make the necessary revisions to her trust and amend it to ensure that his inheritance would go to a trustee to distribute for his benefit rather than directly to him, so as not to impact the assistance he was getting.

With our team of Woman's Worth® life planning professionals, we also look at your tax returns, as tax structures change. We look at the validation of that lifestyle plan. Has there been anything in your lifestyle that might derail the plan because we didn't know about it a year ago? We also look at the income plan. Many times we prematurely lose our jobs, or all of a sudden we find ourselves in the middle of an ugly, unexpected divorce. The plan we might have developed as a couple no longer applies, so we need to re-plan. And, more important, I encourage women in this situation to get a financial physical before a divorce is finalized to ensure they are protected with the strategies they need, and that those are included in the divorce decree, particularly regarding retirement accounts, protection of spousal and child support, etc.

We have to examine every component that would have any impact on the quality of our future financial life, and we want to make the changes today, in a proactive manner, so we're not reacting down the line. Having to react to sudden changes can really affect you physically as well as emotionally, and we'll talk about that in a later section.

We also will look at your asset management plan. Are your investments still right for you, given where you are? What's the economic environment today that will require you to modify the plan? Was there an unexpected debilitating illness or other health issue that changed your life that requires you to regroup?

As you can see, it's very important that you take into account all of these things to ensure that your income plan, your legal documents, and your asset allocations all represent your wishes and desires as you move forward.

I highly recommend that you seek guidance in your journey toward the creation of a life plan that better ensures that you will be prepared financially for the future. As you seek support, it is important that any plan developed is a goal-based plan, with those goals being yours, as unique to you as your DNA, and not the goals of a financial planner, investment adviser, life coach, or estate planning attorney, or even a divorce attorney who may negotiate your financial settlement during a divorce. No cookie-cutter plans will work — your plan is not your favorite one-size-fits-all sweatshirt; nor are those kind of plans acceptable to protect you. I mentioned the problems that financial stress can have on your health, and in the next section we'll cover the importance of your physical and emotional health and the impact these have on your financial well-being, because, ladies, *it's more than the money — it's about total well-being!*

Protecting and Preserving Your Health: What Does It Have To Do With Money?

CHAPTER FIVE

The Health/Wealth Connection

"Health is a state of complete physical, mental and social well-being, and not merely the absence of disease or infirmity."
– World Health Organization, 1948

Remember earlier in the book when we talked about women's increasing longevity? A long life is a great thing, provided your health is good too. But with longer life comes the greater likelihood that at some point you'll face more debilitating illnesses, particularly if you've let your health slide. And with those illnesses come bigger medical expenses that can potentially devastate our carefully made income plans. That's why we want to ensure that in our 50s and 60s we start really taking care of preserving both our physical and emotional health, so it doesn't have such a devastating impact on our wealth. I'm reminded of a quote from something I was reading a while back; it struck me with enormous truth. In essence, someone was being interviewed about longevity, and their response was: "If I knew I'd live in my body this long, I would have taken better care of myself." I've held that close to my mind and my heart, and it defines my financial, emotional, and physical decision-making.

As we look at the statistics, we find close to ¾ of nursing home residents are women. We've acknowledged in previous sections that we are already starting our retirement years with fewer assets, and that we are going to need more assets because of higher-cost living arrangements (i.e., independent living communities, skilled nursing facilities, etc.) that we may find ourselves needing as we move into the second and third phases of our more mature or senior years. It's no secret that women spend more on health care — in fact, before the Affordable Care Act (which made gender-based health insurance ratings illegal), women were routinely charged 50 percent more for monthly health insurance premiums than men.[27] Data generated by the National Committee for Quality Assurance (NCQA) from the Agency for Healthcare Research and Quality (AHRQ) reveals that the disparity and the quality gaps are particularly associated with conditions that are linked with the onset of menopause, so all these health care issues are generated as we move into that life transition. Not only do women experience a mental and emotional transition, but there is a significant physical transition that is going to ultimately impact our financial health and well-being.

When we look at the management of cardiovascular disease, breast cancer, osteoporosis, and menopause in women, it is clear that medical practice patterns are not meeting acceptable standards of care. Let's look at one more thing before we move into the focus of this chapter, and that is the fact that the overall spending on prescription drugs for women through last year was $6.93 billion, versus $5.77 billion for men.

---

[27] Rose Rimler. Healtline. June 13, 2016. "Should Women Pay More for Healthcare Services?" http://www.healthline.com/health-news/should-women-pay-more-health care-services#1. Accessed March 1, 2017.

Women over 50 have a 46 percent risk for developing cardiovascular disease over the course of their remaining lifetime.[28] Also, the probability of being diagnosed with breast cancer, the most commonly diagnosed cancer in women, more than doubles from age 40 to 60.[29] The leading causes for mortality in women today are cardiovascular disease and cancer, and they account for approximately 44 percent of women's deaths in the United States.[30] As we get older, the risk of developing osteoporosis increases after menopause, which brings many additional side complications, like falling and fractures, leading to more health care expense needs.

We need to think about all of this in the context of our total well-being, which is what we are going to cover here. All of these health-oriented issues have an impact on our financial well-being. We have to learn to take care of ourselves. We have to keep our lives in balance: mentally, emotionally, physically, and financially. And, as important, don't forget your spiritual health. Basically, we have to get involved in knowing ourselves and empowering ourselves to be more effective when it comes to how we utilize health care services and how we introduce and fund preventive maintenance resources to ensure that total well-being.

Dr. Christiane Northrup, the author of "Women's Bodies, Women's Wisdom," has identified five of the biggest health mistakes women make, and has advice on how to avoid them. I would like to summarize her insights here.

---

[28] Carolyn J. Crandall. Medicine.net. "Heart Disease in Women." http://www.medicinenet.com/script/main/art.asp?articlekey=11014. Accessed March 2, 2017.

[29] National Cancer Institute. "Breast Cancer Risk in American Women." https://www.cancer.gov/types/breast/risk-fact-sheet. Accessed March 2, 2017.

[30] Centers for Disease Control and Prevention. 2014. "Leading Causes of Death (LCOD) in Females United States, 2014 (current listing)." https://www.cdc.gov/women/lcod/2014/index.htm. Accessed March 2, 2017.

The *first* mistake she identifies is to assume that "the doctors know my body better than I do." The truth is that we as women know our bodies better than anyone else. All too often, when we go to our doctors we forget to tell them what's important, because they may act like they don't have time for us to be there. A doctor is seeing 30 or 35 patients a day, and often seems to be subtly signaling (or not so subtly) that we're wasting his or her valuable time. When we don't tell the doctor what's happening with our bodies, we have to assume that the exam or the medical testing is going to provide him or her with the information he or she needs to treat us. But the truth is that we are able to influence the treatment protocol more effectively than doctors can, if we don't freeze up when we have those opportunities to share information with them, when we have that precious 30 or so minutes with them in the office. It's important to ensure that we are the leaders and the facilitators of the quality of our own health care, not our doctors. We must insist on quality time and quality dialogue about our health.

The *second* mistake Dr. Northrup identifies is the notion many of us have that drugs and surgery are the best approaches to medical problems. We just talked about how much greater are the medical expenses that we can anticipate as women in comparison to men. Standard Western medicine is based on a very limited understanding of the mind-body connection. It's important to recognize that other, alternative medical philosophies are out there, and that they can help us to overcome some of those medical issues without having to rely on advancing the agenda and profits of the pharmaceutical industry. For instance, if we have a headache, we are quick to pop aspirin; if we think that we get migraines, we are quick to go to a physician and try to get help for them. We get depressed and, as women, sometimes we automatically go to those "designer" antidepressants: Prozac and all the other generations of drugs that sedate emotions and feelings. We have to look at alternative treatment protocols that are more effective, and we will talk in the next section about how many medical issues are impacted by emotional and mental types of issues.

Twenty-nine years ago, when I was 36, I was diagnosed with breast cancer. I knew that the cancer was a symptom of something else, because there was no history of cancer in our family at all. My mother lived until age 93, my great aunt lived a bit beyond 100, and several grandparents lived past 100. The medical system that I put myself in wanted quick surgery, quick chemotherapy, then radiation, followed by hormone therapy — but I said, "Stop. I have to really understand why I got this." In those treatment protocols, they offered me a symptomatic solution to my cancer. I needed a systemic solution, because I did not want to add myself to the recurrence statistics.

I took charge of my health problem, contrary to the advice of orthodox physicians. I said, "No, I'm going to research it." I did my research and I found a program that was a metabolic treatment program. I found a physician — an M.D. whose specialization was immunology and who practiced alternative medicine, because I wanted to integrate Western medicine with alternative medicine. This physician (his website is www.dr-gonzalez.com) was located in New York City and I live in Florida, but distance didn't matter, because it was my life that was at risk. He gave me a treatment plan for my cancer that provided a systemic protocol and solution to cancer, not a symptomatic solution. Twenty-nine years later, I am totally cancer-free, because I took charge and I did not listen to the orthodox medical practitioners. So the message here is that we have to take charge of our own health, because we know our own bodies better than anyone else. You see, I knew that my cancer was caused by my intense lifestyle, the toll my caregiving responsibilities had taken on me, and my intense professional career. Put all those risk factors together and I was bound to get something!

The **third** mistake women make, according to Dr. Christiane Northrup, is believing, "My female body is a lemon, and I was born to suffer from menstrual cramps, PMS, excruciating labor pains, and a miserable menopause." Many women do suffer from these health issues, but the fact is that these are normal processes to go through, and they are not designed to result in significant pain and suffering. God didn't create us that way. It's just that we have more pain and suffering when there are some other issues that are creating or magnifying it.

I have learned from my personal experience that the body is designed to heal itself, and that God created this amazing machine that has the ability to self-repair as long as it's properly nourished and its balance is maintained. But too often we are not utilizing what is innate within us when, if we were armed with a little knowledge and information, we could directly influence the quality and quantity of our lives. We are just giving in to what we are being conditioned to believe and what we've been told by the traditional medical system, and we accept it without question — which is quite problematic.

I see this so often with my clients when we are doing their lifestyle plans. They tell me, "My mother died at 70 from a heart attack," or, "My father had diabetes, so I am going to get it; I am going to be a victim." This is the **fourth** mistake: thinking that a bad family history automatically predestines your future health. You might have a predisposition to a certain condition or disease, but it is not inevitable that you will end up with that disease. The truth is, as much as 90 percent of cancers are lifestyle related and have nothing to do with our heredity, and nothing to do with what diseases our parents had.[31] It stands to reason that since 80 to

---

[31] Ariana Eunjung Cha. The Washington Post. Dec. 17, 2015. "Study: Up to 90 percent of cancers not 'bad luck,' but due to lifestyle choices, environment." https://www.washingtonpost.com/news/to-your-health/wp/2015/12/17/study-up-to-

90 percent of all diseases are related to stress and life challenges, if I were to manage my stress and have a healthy lifestyle, then I could turn my genetic statistics around. Often, environmental issues are causing our diseases, not our genes. The question for us is, do we want to be a victim of that, or do we want to be a victor and take charge of it?

The *fifth* mistake (and this is amazing to me, as I journey through my senior years) is the notion that it's normal to get aches and pains and medical problems as we age. Yes, it may be common to do so, but it's not natural and it is not inevitable. The more we stay active, the more we nurture our bodies with proper nutrition for the various stages of our lives, the more we think positively, and the more we hang around with healthy, positive people, the stronger mind-body connection we'll have, and it's not inevitable that we are going to get those aches and pains. We can be in control of the quality and outcome of our health.

Let's take as an example my mother, who lived to 93. When she was 86, the doctors told me as her primary caregiver to take her to hospice, because she had congestive heart failure and they couldn't do anything for her but keep her comfortable. She went from being in apparently great health to being diagnosed with congestive heart failure in a matter of 48 hours, and was sent off to hospice care; the medical system wrote her off without knowing her as a person. I was thinking, "Well, now, that's interesting. My knowledge about congestive heart failure is that this can be managed." But they weren't looking at her, her passion for life, or the strength of her mind; they were looking at her age. She was 86, and they simply decided that they were not going to waste their time with a woman who was 86.

90-of-cancers-not-bad-luck-but-due-to-lifestyle-choices-environment/?utm_term=.85e746fdc2f6. Accessed March 2, 2017.

Well, my mother was an independent, very strong-willed and passionate woman. She had lived as a widow, caring for her family, her grandchildren, her daughters and her sons-in-law, nieces, nephews, and friends; she lived for her family and friends, and this gave her life tremendous meaning. She had a very purposeful existence, had a spirit of hospitality, and had deep social connections, even though at 86 she'd become very ill. And the bottom line, after extensive discussion with her, was that she opted to have surgery to have an aortic valve replacement with a quadruple bypass (two major surgeries in one procedure). At first the doctors refused, saying that they would never do surgery of that extent and nature on an 86-year-old with a severe case of congestive heart failure. But, despite her age and illness, she was a strong woman mentally, and she very effectively confronted her cardiovascular surgeon and said, "Look. I want the surgery because I am not going to live like this. I have had a wonderful life, and I have a wonderful family. If I am going to die, I want to die now on the operating table, because I'm not going to live like this. If God wants me to live, then I'll live through the surgery." Because she was of totally sound mind, the cardiologist had no choice but to do the surgery. He warned me that she would not be able to live independently or regain her strength. He didn't know my mother like I knew her!

So she had the surgery and ultimately had seven beautiful years after that. She defied all medical statistics and all medical standards. Why? Because of her mindset and her passion to continue serving her family and her friends. She still felt like she had a purpose in her life. She wanted to see her grandchildren and her nieces and nephews get married. Her whole heart and soul and passion were dedicated to being there for those grandkids, because that was what she lived for. And never once until the day she died did she put herself in a wheelchair — because she had no intention of giving up her mobility. During those seven years, she broke a hip, and she ended up having pins and rods in her hips, and still recuperated due to her will — still without ever getting into a wheel-chair. The doctors all said that she'd never get up and walk again. But you know what? She got up and walked. Why did she defy medical statistics? It was the power of her mind, and a connection with her passion and her commitment to what her purpose was, and that was her family and her continued service to her family and friends.

We have an opportunity to be proactive in maintaining our physical and emotional health as we are thinking about our retirement years so that we can be certain we get the most out of them. Remember, the most critical influences on our financial health are our physical health, our emotional health, and our mental and spiritual health. All of those packaged together are going to have a direct influence on the strength of our financial health. Why would we want to plan for increased health care costs in our senior years when we can mitigate health issues with proper balance in our current lives?

There are many similarities between health and financial issues. Behavior changes can significantly improve women's health and finances. The following table provides several insights and examples of the health-wealth connection.

HEALTH-WEALTH CONNECTION		
Similarities	Health	Wealth
Problem generally starts small	Weight gain starts small: three to four pounds a year. The U.S. Department of Agriculture found the caloric intake of American adults rose from 1,854 to 2,002 calories a day in the past 20 years.	Debt balances on credit cards, interest rates, and fees on outstanding balances rise gradually. Add penalties with late payments or exceeding the credit limit, and what was a small credit issue balloons into a large one.
Lots of technical jargon	A study recently found half of American adults have heightened risks for health complications due to trouble following instructions on drug labels or from their doctor. Patients also receive contradictory "expert" opinions from medical practitioners and research results. What was a medical miracle yesterday causes the cancer of tomorrow.	Comprehending investing terms and personal finance language is a challenge, particularly for women who weren't socialized with financial discipline. Getting opinions from five different financial professionals who speak different financial languages could yield five different financial strategies.

Fear of drastic changes	Most people believe a major life change is required for optimal health. It's more important and effective to just get started one step at a time — take the stairs instead of the elevator or switch one processed snack for a piece of fruit.	Some people fear never having enough money saved for retirement because of gloomy economic reports and hearing they need millions of dollars to retire. Instead, start small: Save $1 a day or 1 percent of your earnings and then build from there.
Lack of limits causes problems	The more food we are served, the more we eat ("supersizing" our meals).	The more credit we're extended through credit cards and different lines of credit, the more we spend.
Longevity connection	Those who practice healthy behaviors (not smoking, eating vegetables, etc.) decrease their risk of dying prematurely and increase the quality of their elder years.	The cost of managing health care creates the need for more wealth to ensure you don't outlive your assets.
People expect quick fixes	There are no miracle cures of the kind claimed in infomercials or media: "Lose 30 pounds in 30 days," "magic cream removes wrinkles," etc.	"Guaranteed" investment returns at rates higher than historical averages or no obvious relationship between risk and reward.

Need for routine checkups	Medical screenings such as blood pressure checks, mammograms, bone-density tests, and colonoscopies are important to ensure optimal health and prevent/manage debilitating diseases.	Financial checkups are equally important as we age; a financial checkup can help "diagnose" problems before they get worse, uncover risk, find exposure, or evaluate progress toward your financial goals.
Positive mental attitude	If you expect to succeed in your health habits, you will succeed. Expectation produces results, and results are powerful motivators (i.e., pounds lost, lower BMI).	Again, if you expect to succeed and positively confront your savings plan, you will succeed (i.e., "I can save $50 per month now, and later, when my credit card is paid off, I can save more").
Ongoing maintenance required	Your health should never be taken for granted and requires "maintenance" activities to develop lifetime habits (i.e., eating nutritious meals, regular exercise, etc.).	Financial maintenance includes consistently saving for retirement and beefing up emergency funds.

Source: O'Neill, Barbara, PhD, CFP, and Ensle, Karen, EdD, RD, Rutgers Cooperative Extension. "Health and Wealth Connections." http://njaes.rutgers.edu/sshw/.

Financial worries are making women sick. The health-wealth connection isn't just a matter of keeping our health; it's about how we were divinely designed as women and who we are. Most women have a great need for safety and security, for certainty, for predictability. In our more mature years and as we move into our senior years, we might suddenly face some devastating life event. I will never forget the clients whom I recently helped divide their estate and assets because they were in their early 70s and they were going through a divorce after a 51-year marriage. These life events have a significant impact and, as such, introduce enormous financial stressors. I still work with the woman who was a victim of this process. Not surprisingly, she started experiencing significant physical issues after the divorce. When I sat down and talked with her, it was immediately evident to me that her financial stress and worries contributed at least in part to her physical problems. After resolving her financial needs, she was better positioned to focus on her physical self, and her health issues dissipated.

Medical professionals confirm: financial stress causes significant physical and psychological discomfort. It leads to anxiety, which leads to depression, which in turn leads to high blood pressure, which leads to stroke.[32, 33] We have to face the reality of addressing the financial stress head-on, because if we ignore the problem by pretending things aren't really bad, the financial stress gets greater. That leads to greater health issues, and then we get more financial stress. You can see how this vicious cycle will create a downward spiral of financial stress and poor health.

---

[32] New York Times. "Health Guide: Stress and Anxiety." http://www.nytimes.com/health/guides/symptoms/stress-and-anxiety/possible-complications.html. Accessed April 10, 2017.

[33] Cambridge Credit Counseling Corp. "Financial Stress and Your Health." https://www.cambridge-credit.org/financial-stress-and-your-health.html. Accessed April 10, 2017.

It seems like every year I see studies that illustrate the impact on our health of the financial woes that we as women can have. One study reported in 2010 by Health, titled "Financial Woes Add Anxiety to Breast Cancer Diagnosis," followed 487 women with breast cancer and showed that financial pressure put low- and medium-income women at higher risk for the kinds of anxiety and depression I just talked about. While that article may be out of date, physicians estimate that 75-90 percent of all doctor visits are stress-related.[34] That stress can lead to costs associated with medical treatment, which in turn creates more financial hardship and stress. It's a vicious cycle. And we can control this vicious cycle that robs us of a dignified retirement.

How can we diminish the stress and the health challenges it creates for us as women? First I would encourage you to deal with the money question, because so much of that stress is attached to our worries about being able to take care of ourselves, or, more appropriately stated, our fear of becoming destitute. We worry about money, and we worry about our kids. What we see and read in the media only exacerbates our stress; it seems like every day brings us nothing but more bad news. There is a recession, there are no jobs, the stock market is a white-knuckle roller-coaster ride; all this relentless negativity creates fear and doubt in our minds, and we allow that messaging to contaminate our peace and sanity. How many people listen to the news and walk away with a warm, fuzzy feeling? More likely it seems like doom and gloom, and that's exactly what we don't need. Turn off the TV, get off the Internet, and don't let yourself be pulled into that apocalyptic mindset. You are in control of your destiny, not the media.

---

[34] WebMD. "The Effects of Stress on Your Body." http://www.webmd.com/balance/stress-management/effects-of-stress-on-your-body. Accessed March 2, 2017.

We have to take concrete action toward solving our financial problems by creating the type of life plan that I've talked about throughout this book. Putting a plan together gives us relief from anxiety by addressing those scary "what if?" scenarios. The major objective of this plan is to fill in the blanks of ambiguity and replace such ambiguity with facts and data that can be measured and reinforced. "What if I lost my spouse or we lost one source of income?" "What if I have to move into a caregiving role and all of a sudden I can't work anymore?" "I'm 60 and I hadn't planned on retiring until I was 65, but my parents need help."

I had a client just recently tell me, "I have to relocate to Ohio because my parents have nobody around them to help them; my father is 90 and my mother is 80, and I've got to get up there and help them." That's a stressful situation, and required a change in her plans to ensure that she could do this without impacting the quality of her life, both now and in the future.

Also, I urge you to accept your financial reality. Is it really a fact that you do have true financial concerns, or is it just that you're being infected by the culture of fear, fed by bad news in the media?

Let's now talk about income versus expenses. Do we have a handle on our cash flow? I can't tell you how many clients come into my office, and when I ask, "How much do you really need to live on?" I would say eight out of 10 clients don't have any idea what they truly need. How do you manage your money stress and improve the quality of your lifestyle from a health perspective if you don't have a handle on your basic lifestyle expenses?

The next area I'd like to address is negative self-talk. Women tend to really beat themselves up a lot. We tend to focus too much on negatives in what we do, how we look, how much we spend, how unsuccessful we are relative to others, and the list can go on. I encourage you ladies to focus on your financial successes. We have to start affirming what we did right with money, because, even if we like to shop and continue to have more shoes and clothes than we need, there is always something positive to focus on. We need to get over the negative and affirm what small steps have been made to get these types of threats to our financial security under control.

Finally, and the most relevant from my perspective, we've got to stop fortune-telling about our money problems. We are constantly predicting the negative and reacting to it. If you think negatively, not only are you going to have negative personality dispositions, but you are going to inadvertently end up creating some medical issues and more financial problems for yourself. We've got to balance living in the moment while we are preparing for the future. It's essential that we look at ways to cope and maintain balance through proper self-care.

The mission at Woman's Worth® is to help you create a life plan that balances your emotional, physical, and financial well-being. Money matters don't have to make you sick if you stick to your life plan, which should be the cornerstone of total well-being.

CHAPTER SIX

Taking Care of No. 1

"Let food be thy medicine, and medicine be thy good."
– Hippocrates

L et's shift the focus to addressing lifestyles, and how a healthy lifestyle can not only boost our longevity but our vitality as we live into our 80s and 90s. Who wants to be 85 and be merely half-alive?

A Harvard research study about women and longevity concluded that women who don't smoke, who maintain a healthy weight, who eat a healthful diet, and who get regular exercise reduce their risk of dying from any cause, particularly from heart disease and cancer, the two biggest threats to women's mortality. Did we really need a study to tell us that? I'd say that's already fairly evident to us, because as women we read about those things constantly in all the women's magazines and journals we pick up at the grocery or bookstores. The bookstores are full of books about this, but are we embracing the message?

But the numbers are more impressive than you might think. Here are the amazing results that Harvard released in 2008: by adopting these lifestyle changes, women reduced their overall risk of death by 55 percent. They reduced their risk of dying of cancer by 44 percent, and their risk of dying from heart disease by 72 percent.[35] What this tells us is that, as empowered and wise women, we can take control of our health by taking control of four significant lifestyle changes. Not smoking and maintaining a healthy diet, healthy weight, and regular physical activity help us reduce the risk of dying prematurely. We are wise women, empowered to control our destiny with vigor and vitality. We have control over the quality of our lives. We have control over our destiny, and we have control over our root-cause emotions that might be getting in our way. We can have lower medical expenses. We could certainly have less financial stress. So what does this mean in terms of personal action?

It is essential to incorporate healthy foods and exercise into each day at a simple level. When we are having difficult or challenging times — perhaps we lost the job, we lost the income from a spouse, or we are under other stress — that is not a time to spend less money on fresh produce. That is not the time to cut out our gym membership. It's a time to be proactive in incorporating more of those healthy lifestyle practices and choices into our routines to help ourselves to better manage the life event stress and maintain optimal health.

The health-wealth connection requires that you create life balance. You've got to proactively seek happiness. When you're assessing your life balance, you need to look at yourself in the context of your finances, your social connections, and also your spiritual connections. Are you fulfilled in the spiritual realm? How

---

[35] Rob van Dam, Tricia Li, Donna Spiegelman, Oscar H. Franco, Frank B. Hu. Harvard. BMJ. "Combined impact of lifestyle factors on mortality: prospective cohort study in US women." 2008; 337:a 1440. https://www.researchgate.net/publication/23260903_Combined_impact_of_lifestyle_factors_on_mortality_Prospective_cohort_study_in_US_women. Accessed March 2, 2017.

about in the area of relationships; are you loved by the people who mean the most to you? Are you ensuring that all the relationships in your life are positive, constructive relationships that are free of any toxicity?

These components represent the critical puzzle pieces that make up the complete "you." The more that all of these factors are healthy, integrated, and aligned with your personal desires and passions, the greater the likelihood that you will see optimal improvement in your physical and emotional health. What does it take to make changes? First and foremost, it takes clarity. We need to get a realistic vision for our lives. It doesn't matter whether I am 50, 60, or 80; I need to be clear on the vision that I have for the rest of my life. Getting clarity on that vision really helps in taking the first step to making the proper changes. It requires self-awareness: understanding why I am where I am, and taking responsibility for that. We didn't get where we are in our lives by accident; we put ourselves here. Let's accept responsibility, and let go of any anger or frustration that might be getting in the way of our ability to move from where we are today to where we want to be, to achieve that vision for our lives. A commitment is so important in all areas that influence total well-being: making a commitment to emotional changes, a commitment to the physical changes we have to make, and a commitment to the financial changes that we have to make. All of these are essential, and they are interdependent on one another, because we were created as one — body, mind, and spirit.

There's a quote by comedian and actor Jackie Mason that I love, because it really goes to the heart of my message: "So many people spend their health gaining their wealth and then have to spend their wealth to regain their health." The cycle is like a little rat running in a wheel and he can't escape. You want to be the rat that escapes and maintains a positive, healthy mindset of well-being.

Dr. Wayne Dyer, in his book "The Secrets for Success and Inner Peace," urges an empowering strategy of optimism and hope, including keeping a mind that's "open to everything and attached to nothing" — including your own life story — and valuing your "divinity." Dyer seems to encourage a kind of internal revolution, claiming "you can't solve a problem with the same mind that created it" and suggesting you avoid "resentments" and "thoughts that weaken you." It's a book worth reading and a message worth carrying with you.

Your commitment is your recipe for the total well-being that gives us that beautiful balance between our health and our wealth. Three things women need to do every year: first, we have to have our annual emotional tune-up. Now, what does that look like? That means giving yourself permission to go on retreats, or getting yourself some life coaching if you can't figure out what your purpose or vision is for your life. If you lost a loved one, it is okay to go to grief counseling. You may need the help of a mental health counselor if you have gone through a devastating life event. Or you may simply need to get away with the gals. I have a precious client who is full of life and vitality, and her secret weapon and mode of balance is "faith, family, and friends." She is a widow in her late 70s. Every year she and five ladies she went to high school with get together for a weeklong holiday retreat. They create their own unique getaway and they are so full of life and joy. She is my hero; I look at her and realize that I want to be just like her at that stage in my own life. She and her friends go on trips abroad, or sometimes they just get a house on a beach somewhere, but they all enjoy life together. Make time for your own weeks or weekends away with the gals.

The second area of importance to our total well-being is that of aligning ourselves with the right coaches (life, business, health, exercise, spiritual, etc.) who can help you maintain objectivity and provide the fuel to a proper life balance. I often use both a business coach and a spiritual director to keep me in balance, because I am a Type A personality and I work a lot. I could easily put in 70 hours a week consistently, which is why I need coaches and other resources to keep me in line with my purpose and vision. Annually, we need to get those emotional tune-ups through venues and resources other than friends and family, because those close to us can rarely be objective due to our emotional connection.

The third item we need to put on our yearly "must-do" list is our annual medical evaluations. We need those complete physicals with preventive diagnostic assessments. We need that wellness coaching. If we think we have tried every diet in the world and we're still struggling with our weight, we might need a guide to help us go through an improvement process to regain our wellness. We need to make the time to engage in various health assessments and preventive assessments as well as behavioral assessments, because the root cause of an illness or medical problem can often be mental or emotional.

Obviously, we need our annual financial checkup, which was discussed previously. A financial physical provides an in-depth assessment of where we are against where we want to be from this point forward. It's important for us to make sure we make those commitments. The quality of our lives, our total well-being, depends on focusing on all of these areas, our emotions, our physical health, and our financial health. Our lives literally depend on actively following through with plans and actions that can enhance our longevity. If not, we run the risk of creating significant financial pressures.

CHAPTER SEVEN

What You Can Do
(After You Stop Making Excuses)

"Facing the truth means going beyond just admitting we've done some-thing wrong; it means not making excuses for that wrong behavior."
– Joyce Meyer

Okay, ladies, let's face it: We are conditioned from birth to please. Because of our multiple and many times conflict-ing roles — as daughters, sisters, mothers, grandmothers, wives, employees, caregivers, business owners, and all the subroles within these super-roles — our vitality gets zapped. We lose ourselves and perhaps our dreams, desires, and aspirations, sacrificing them for the good of the family unit or others we are accountable to. Then one day many of us wake up (and I pray we do wake up, as it took me until I was in my mid-50s to be enlight-ened!) and our vitality is zapped!

I couldn't achieve optimal health and total well-being until I seized the opportunity to get away from my stressful career in a major corporation, my responsibilities with a business I owned, and my caregiving responsibilities with an aging parent. I had to create a new mindset that gave me permission to dig deep within myself and awaken the desires I had repressed since my mid-20s. For me it was taking myself out of my environment and cycling through Tuscany, reconnecting with nature, with sounds of stillness, reveling in scents and fragrances unknown to me. On that journey, I gave myself permission to enjoy the present, and this experience birthed a new life purpose within me.

The journey to seek your purpose does not have to be dramatic. Perhaps a simple weekend getaway with friends, a life coaching retreat, a church retreat — something that simply gets you out of your current realm of thinking and gets you to consider the possibilities for a beautiful new life that was designed by our Creator for you and only you.

To begin the transformation, we need to be properly nourished so we can get our blood flowing, our heart pumping, and our brains moving on the creative side. Some of the top experts in the various self-improvement disciplines give the following advice on giving your body the high-quality, true nourishment it needs. Let's face it: what is a life of purpose and passion without a body that is alive and optimally functioning through our elder years?

Here's a "prescription" from a well-known wellness coach, Lucy Buckner, the founder of Easy Wellness Today, for action steps you can take that will revitalize your health on all levels:

1. Truly nourishing exercise — that means exercise you really enjoy. One of my clients uses dance as her truly nourishing exercise so she doesn't have to take on the drudgery of the treadmill or other forms of exercise that don't nourish her spirit. What's yours? Truly nourishing exercise is that which makes you feel totally alive before the exercise, during the exercise, and then afterward. The benefit is that if you love it you won't make excuses to avoid the commitment, so find your nourishing exercise and make it a part of your regular routine.

2. Truly nourishing breathing — breathe right! The most fundamental of all exercises can actually give you more energy and

vitality. We have a life force within us, and when we breathe deeply and consistently, our mental clarity is improved, we reduce anxiety and stress, and thus we approach our lives with greater vitality. Breathing deeply opens the pathways of oxygen to the brain, and this is what we need to live a life of purpose and passion. So anytime you feel stressed, dull, or anxious, take five minutes and do some breathing exercises and you will feel renewed and ready for life. I have a breathing application on my fitness watch. It reminds me frequently to breathe as it's measuring my heart rate. When I take one minute to do a breathing exercise, I see my heart rate reducing and I feel less stressed (and those around me find me more pleasurable to be around!).

3. Truly nourishing food. We have talked about this previously, but I can't stress enough the importance of eating foods right for your body. No two bodies were designed the same, as we all have a unique composition of RNA/DNA. I learned this the hard way on my journey, as I read all the health literature and research and decided that I was going to be a vegetarian, so I was one for seven years. I ended up with the diagnosis no woman wants to hear — breast cancer — and was totally appalled, because I had thought I was eating right, exercising right, etc. What I learned after consulting with a holistic medical professional was that my body tested as a moderate vegetarian metabolizer, with an immune system that needed animal protein in moderate portions. While I had thought I was eating nourishing food, my immune system was depleted, creating a health issue. The doctor surmised that I caused my own cancer by the self-prescribed diet I had pursued for seven years, coupled with the stress I was experiencing in my life that depleted my body of essential nutrients faster than I could replenish them! Know thy body! Never participate in a "one-size-fits-all" diet. Find out what your metabolic type is; don't use a book to find out, or base it on your blood type, but align

yourself with a health coach who will be your guide to resources specific to you.

4. Experiencing pleasure and joy. Increase your joy and pleasure by feeding all of your senses in daily activities. As women juggling so many competing priorities, we typically let life fly by us. We are in intense and stressful careers, fulfilling our responsibilities as heads of our households, worrying about the kids and grandkids, and we miss experiencing the simple pleasures that will give us joyful thoughts. I was talking to a girlfriend and she was mentioning how stressed she was and how tired she was all the time, working and keeping up with her home and preparing meals for her husband, and being a good grandmother with babysitting duties. What was amazing to me was that she said she was sitting on her patio one day and saw three deer come into her yard, and she silenced her mind by focusing on the three deer and staying present in that moment, where she connected with nature and its beauty. Moments like these, when we allow ourselves to experience natural joy through all of our senses, optimize our health and feelings of well-being. And they don't cost a penny! So allow yourself to feel the air on your face with a bike ride, smell the vegetation on your next casual walk, listen to the ocean, hear the birds sing, listen to the crickets, etc.

Interestingly, over the last year we have seen more and more research coming out about the connection between stress and women's health, and that the majority of the stress is financially induced stress.

There's also been research that shows that stress increases the risk of metabolic syndrome.[36] And what is metabolic syndrome? It

---

[36] Janczura, M., Bochenek, G., Nowobilski, R., Dropinski, J., Kotula-Horowitz, K., Laskowicz, B., ... Domagala, T. PLoS One. 2015. "The Relationship of Metabolic Syndrome with Stress, Coronary Heart Disease and Pulmonary Function - An Occupational

is the increase of abdominal fat that creates insulin resistance and ultimately Type 2 diabetes, which leads to heart disease. Typically, if you've got Type 2 diabetes, you are at a higher risk for heart disease. Researchers found that those who showed clinical signs of metabolic syndrome were more likely to have experienced a great deal of financial-, work-, and health-related stress. Financial stress and work-related stress were also found to be significantly more likely to lead to certain conditions, such as cardiac issues, obesity, high cholesterol, and also insulin resistance.

I want to discuss one more bit of compelling research that I am following, particularly as I see trends in my own financial practice: the number of single, divorced, and widowed women who are approaching their elder years alone. With 18 percent of seniors living alone, 43 percent of older Americans (which amounts to 20 million of us, by the way) suffer from chronic loneliness.[37] That is unbelievable — 20 million of us suffer from chronic loneliness? Loneliness has been reported to have broad and very profound health effects. Because of its magnitude, loneliness is now recognized as a distinct mental health issue. Medical researchers are also finding that chronic loneliness correlates with increases in the incidence of diabetes and sleep disorders, and puts older people at a greater risk for high blood pressure and other life-threatening problems, like a weakened immune system, as well as Alzheimer's disease.

If we are going to face our senior years alone, the message for us is that social connections are critical to maintaining optimal health. There are ways we can cure chronic loneliness and lower

---

Cohort-Based Study." 10(8), e0133750. http://doi.org/10.1371/journal.pone.0133750. Accessed March 2, 2017.

[37] Anne-Marie Botek. AgingCare.com. "The Elder Loneliness Epidemic." https://www.agingcare.com/articles/loneliness-in-the-elderly-151549.htm. Accessed March 2, 2017.

our health risk. I will share a few thoughts on that. First of all, it is important to nurture our personal relationships. Do not substitute electronic communication for face-to-face interactions. The highest users of Facebook are women over 50, and while that is a good electronic form of communication, it cannot be a substitute for quality face-to- face contact.

Take time to volunteer rather than just sitting at home. Volunteer in areas that put you around other people. Libraries always need people to help out with shelving or other tasks. Many elementary schools like to have guest readers come in for story time. Join a social club or a community organization to get involved and stay involved. If you like adventure and international travel, what about the Peace Corps, which has programs that encourage retirees to volunteer? What about Seniors on a Mission, which is a nonprofit that coordinates mission trips for seniors? And, we've seen an emergence of Meetup groups. Meetup is an online social networking portal that facilitates offline group meetings in various localities around the world. Meetup allows members to find and join groups based on common interests like politics, books, games, movies, health, pets, careers, or hobbies. If you don't find something you like to do with an existing group, then start one in your own area. No excuses for social isolation! Or, if you are inclined to reach out and help communities experiencing disasters, get trained as a first responder on a disaster recovery team. If you are retired from a career, stay connected with your former colleagues. Frequently our families are spread all over the continental United States or even globally, so it's hard to stay in touch with family. That makes it even more essential that we put an effort into maintaining social relationships.

I can't overemphasize how essential it is to educate ourselves about loneliness, because far too often we might not realize that we are lonely, because it's our habitual state. I am an introvert, and because I have a lot of social connections through my profession, when I am not at work I want to lock myself in a corner in my home, read my books, do my research, and be alone. But I know that's not good, so I force myself to make the effort to stay connected with my friends and my colleagues in order to ensure that I have a quality social balance.

We are all going to have difficult times as we age, especially when we start seeing those people we care about, our loved ones, our close friends, all start passing away (or, as some folks prefer, "crossing the ocean"). There are things we can do to cope during these difficult times, and so I'm going to wrap up by saying that if you are stressing over finances and creating health challenges for yourself, get realistic about your finances, because there is not a problem that cannot be solved in that realm. Stay positive and in control. A defeatist attitude is our worst enemy when it comes to our health. Try using the following affirmations on a daily basis, because if you can confess it, you can possess it!

Affirmations for Being an Elder of Excellence
By Louise Hay

I have my whole life ahead of me.
I am young and beautiful... at every age.
I contribute to society in fulfilling and productive ways.
I am in charge of my finances, my health, and my future.
I am respected by all whom I come in contact with.
I honor and respect the children and adolescents in my life.
I greet each new day with energy and joy.
I live every day to the fullest.
I sleep well at night.
I think new and different thoughts each day.
My life is a glorious adventure.
I am open to experiencing all that life has to offer.
My family is supportive of me, and I am supportive of them.
I have no limitations.

I speak up; my voice is heard by the leaders in society.
I take the time to play with my inner child.
I meditate, take quiet walks, and enjoy nature; I enjoy
spending time alone.
Laughter is a big part of my life; I hold nothing back.
I think of ways to help heal the planet, and I implement them.
I contribute to the harmony of life.
I have all the time in the world.
My later years are my treasure years.

Health and wealth are critical resources for living a happy, ful-filled, and successful life. People in poor health tend to die prema-turely. Additionally, they spend thousands of dollars on health care that could have been used for other things. On the other hand, women who practice proper and recommended health be-haviors generally exceed the average life expectancy. Of course, we need a larger nest egg to ensure that we don't outlive our re-sources. But that is where we can shift spending to those things that we love to do with our families, with our loved ones, versus spending it on mental health professionals or spending it in the medical system.

We know that our health and our personal finances are directly associated with our level of happiness, and research data indicates that four factors strongly predict happiness and well-being — and this is across the board, in all cultures studied. Those factors are health, economic status, employment, and family relationships.

I'd like to share with you a client's story as it relates to the con-nection between stress and physical health. This woman was a young widow who had to go back to work after her husband's sudden death. The only job she could find was a very stressful one with a large corporation, collecting on credit card debts. She had to go back to work concurrently as she was trying to cope with the emotional pain of losing her mate, and dealing with her equally devastated 12-year-old daughter. She went from being totally healthy to suffering from a series of health issues and crises, experiencing all types of symptoms and illnesses. She was not overweight or out of shape, and was a young 52 when I first met her, four years after this tragic life event. But all of a sudden she started having sinus issues, she was plagued with chronic flus and viruses, and her energy was sapped by it all. Not surprisingly, her poor health started creating emotional issues, and she got on a vicious cycle where she was very unhealthy, both physically and emotionally.

She woke up one day and realized it was her job that was making her sick, and she felt as though she wasn't going to be living long if she didn't do something about it. So she quit her job, determined to find something part-time that she could feel passionate about. Shortly after she quit her job, over the next 30 days she began seeing significant improvements in her health. Just by removing that one stressor, she saw a significant improvement in her health. Of course, it created a new stress in that she had to consider the loss of income, and had to live off of her assets. But even though she had a competing stressor, it was not as significant, and she could manage it, because she could control it better than the negative impact of poor health.

Just recently, I saw her in my office and she had remarried. She got a horse, which was always her passion, and her health continued to be at optimal levels. She is totally off of every medication she was on and has taken a holistic approach; she is eating right and exercising consistently. She has satisfied her emotional needs by getting a pet, which happened to be the horse that she can ride, that she can go feed, that she can pay attention to. She has nurtured her social relationships in reconnecting with the old high school sweetheart whom she married. She looks like she is about 10 years younger and a completely different human being. It didn't happen until she took charge. She just decided that she was sick and tired of being sick and tired. When the price associated with not changing exceeded the price associated with change, true change occurred.

Let's talk about nourishing our body to maintain its optimal health. One of the first components is obviously nutrition. Proper nutrition rules our vitality, because it is essential for energy. We should consider food as the fuel for this amazing machine that is our body. The food we eat can either give us energy or it can deplete our energy completely.

When I talk about food, I am not referring to dieting. I have been taught by my health coach, Lucy Buckner, to take the word "diet" out of my vocabulary, so now I do not believe in dieting. Lucy also taught me that the problem with women and dieting is that anytime the word "diet" is used, that means restriction (she makes a special note of the fact that, within the word itself is the word "die," which has a negative connotation). That puts more stress on us, because if I violate this diet, I beat myself up. I create more emotional anxiety, and thus put myself into this vicious cycle of poor mind, body, and spirit health. If we can look at nutrition as that essential fuel for our bodies to provide us with energy, and we don't have to worry about dieting, we can optimize our proper weight. If you struggle in this area, a health coach can be your moral support and guide you toward changing your mindset. Plus, in the age of the internet, there are multiple resources and communities available to help us that are specific to our unique needs.

What are ways in which you can boost your vitality? We talked about it earlier: first and foremost are whole and real foods. We live in an instant society. We want instant gratification with everything. We want quick foods, we want processed foods, and we want instant oatmeal, instant potatoes, instant coffee, etc. We want instant this, instant that. The problem is that anytime there is "instant," anytime there is fat, it means processed. Anytime you're talking processed food, it means that it is very bad for you, because it is loaded with many chemicals and poor nutrients that don't boost our vitality. In fact, it accelerates the zapping of your vitality!

I know this firsthand, because when I went on my cancer treatment program I began a clinically developed diet that consisted of 60 percent raw fruits and vegetables, and 40 percent whole grains. The only animal protein in my diet was two to three servings per week of soft proteins, such as eggs or deep-sea fish (excluding all shellfish). That diet gives me tons of energy, energy that allows me to work these 60- and 70-hour weeks and continue a good exercise protocol, so I'm a prime example of how whole, real foods give us vitality. The closer what you eat is to its natural state, the more nutrients or fuel it's going to give your body. So the more raw stuff you eat, the better, and we want to eat an abundance of fresh fruits and vegetables. The other key to good health is drinking plenty of water. Water is not only important in helping us to have healthy-looking skin, but it is essential for the body to absorb the nutrients we are giving it.

Many health plans advocate for an optimal eating habit of eating every two hours. That boosts the efficiency of how our body digests food, so it is important that we get away from this ingrained habit of having three big meals a day, and switch to eating smaller meals every two hours. What frequently happens with women is that we put ourselves on these deceptive diets — the "lose 30 pounds in 30 days" kind of things — that dictate what and when we eat, and often we find ourselves hungry. The problem is that if your diet leaves you feeling hunger pangs, that is a really bad sign. It means that your body is storing anything that you put into it as fat. And we don't want that, because when we start experiencing the estrogen loss associated with menopause, we start developing abdominal fat. That's because we are not putting the proper nutrients in our bodies. Instead of going on another fad diet, try a good blend of healthy foods — "live" proteins (such as unprocessed, lean meats) and a piece of fruit or a vegetable or one of the more complex carbohydrates — eaten in smaller amounts every two hours. You'll find that your hunger pangs go away and your vitality increases. And remember to take the word "diet" out of your vocabulary.

Eliminate the three great white killers: white flour, sugar, and saturated fats, including lard. The other thing to avoid is processed food. Anything that you purchase already prepared with a label that tells you it has more than two or three ingredients is filled with chemicals and preservatives, and it is essential that we get away from these products. And ditch anything with the words "diet," "low-fat," or "low-carb" that you gravitate to thinking it's a reduced-calorie food, because it typically is not.

A book that I highly recommend to everyone who really wants to develop good eating habits and drop a lot of weight without having to "go on a diet" is Dr. Joel Fuhrman's "Eat to Live." It presents a food plan that reverses many types of diseases using a holistic approach. You don't even have to go pay hundreds of thousands of dollars to get some advice; Dr. Fuhrman is on public broadcasting, educating people. For information on his website, see the back of this book.

Don't forget proper supplementation. As part of my treatment protocol for cancer, for the first two years I was taking about 150 supplements a day. Now that I am on maintenance, I am down to about 100 supplements a day. If I go into the traditional medical system for a diagnostic check, they look at the list of everything I'm taking, and they tell me I am crazy. They tell me that I am going to a quack, that the supplements aren't doing anything for me, and that I am just wasting my money and flushing money down the toilet. Well, I am a 29-year cancer survivor using a holistic protocol, and they are still saying I'm crazy. Let's not even put any energy into figuring this one out — it's not even worthy of our mental exertion.

That reaction is simply the uninformed voice of traditional Western medicine that has not been enlightened. As the old saying goes, what you are not up on, you are down on. Some Western doctors don't have the knowledge or the education or the training on the value of supplements. They are going to be down on them, because they would rather give out a prescription drug as opposed to encouraging the use of supplements and vitamins that could correct medical issues (see the website for the 24-hour pharmacist at dear-pharmacist.com for nutritional supplement replacements for a wide variety of prescription drugs).

Here's another example from my own personal health experience. When I was 50 years old, all of a sudden I got very sick. I couldn't understand why, because I rarely got sick. I went from being totally healthy to having what was considered to be a serious sinus infection. I live in Florida, where sinus issues are a problem for many people, but I had never had any such issues. I woke up with sinus problems that kept getting worse. I made a big mistake: after more than 20 years of not having put anything synthetic in my body, I took antibiotics, because I just needed a quick fix, as I was going on a business trip. They made me very sick and basically poisoned my body, and I gave new meaning to the phrase "sick as a dog." I ended up going to a specialist because the antibiotics didn't work, and then after three weeks I was even sicker: my ears closed up; my throat closed up. A very dear and precious friend of mine is an internal medicine doctor, and she sent me to another ENT specialist; he gave me a steroid and said I needed surgery. I was thinking, *No, I haven't had any of these problems before in my entire life. Something's wrong.*

But I ended up in the hospital because we couldn't correct it, and they started slamming me with antibiotic IVs, and brought in an infectious disease physician. The more drugs they were putting in me, the sicker I was getting. By now, I could hardly talk, held hostage to this hospital system and getting sicker as I lay in the hospital. I managed to call my doctor in New York, and told him, "There is something wrong. These people are killing me. Will you tell me what's going on?"

When I told him what had happened and gave him the scenario, symptoms, and treatment protocol, he said, "Wow, it sounds like you have an autoimmune disorder. It's viral, and I don't know why they're giving you all of these chemicals, because you are not going to get better. They are just going to make you sicker." Even though he was in New York and I was in Florida, he very quickly diagnosed that I had Epstein-Barr virus, a very advanced stage of mono (which they never would have suspected or diagnosed due to my age). He talked to the local physician and had the hospital discharge me before they killed me, and, boy, was I glad I had a health advocate who understood the immune system.

It turned out that he was right: I had mono. Now, who would have thought someone 50 years old would have a serious case of mono? It was a very severe case. And he prescribed two things: thymus extract, which is a glandular supplement, and a tonic called Super Tonic that's an organic preparation of garlic, cayenne pepper, and a couple of other ingredients that you put into water and drink. He told me that in three days I would be better than new. And within two days, every symptom disappeared and I was back to health. But I had to introduce detoxification protocols to rid my system of the lingering effects of antibiotics. I learned firsthand the dangers of prescription drugs, and have vowed since then never to allow them to enter my body.

I am convinced beyond a shadow of a doubt that I would have died had I stayed in the hospital, because they were treating me with something my body couldn't handle, and I was getting a toxic overload. So, supplements do work and can often replace prescription drugs, but be prudent and use the right kinds of supplements while under the care of a holistic medical practitioner. I do not embrace synthetic supplements. Synthetic supplements create more health issues, because your body can't release and can't utilize them efficiently or over time. Let's be wise women when it comes to what we put in our bodies with supplements, because I would argue, based on my experience, 80 percent of what we pick up in health food stores is pure junk and processed. Just because something says "all natural," it is not necessarily all natural. Educate yourself by reading the labels. If it's got more than two or three ingredients, it is often not natural even though the manufacturers are allowed to call it "all natural." The best course of action is to align yourself with a holistic medical professional who will evaluate your situation and get you the proper supplements.

We also hurt ourselves with the personal care products we put on our bodies, like shampoos and body lotions that have tons of preservatives. Our skin absorbs all these chemicals, and that is the pathway to the cells in your body. You could be putting a lot of good stuff in yourself, you could be eating right, you could be taking the right supplements, you can be drinking your eight glasses of water, you could just be doing all the right things — but guess what? You're potentially undoing all that good by using some cream full of chemicals that promises to make you look younger, or rid you of cellulite. Be thoughtful about the chemicals that are in those things that we think are making us healthy.

Is your environment good for your health? Are you using a lot of cleaning chemicals and toxic kinds of chemicals that you are breathing in? Are your laundry detergents creating skin conditions that lead you to have to take supplements? As we get older, our bodies start transitioning, and what used to work for us when we were 50 — maybe a skincare product or a laundry detergent — may not work for us when we are 70.

It's important for us to come up with a plan for ourselves and do things rationally, systematically, and incrementally. I don't expect you to go from where you are now to where you want to be, overnight. But do take the opportunity to identify, what one thing am I going to do in the next 72 hours after I read this book? What is the one thing that I am going to do to improve some aspect of my health? Just one thing. You nail that down and you go to the next.

Let's talk a little more about exercise, and not in the usual context of going and sweating in a gym for an hour, because, let's face it, most of us have active lives, whether we are working, whether we are retired, whether we are single or married. While I highly recommend the use of a trainer to help you, there are many great resources out there in terms of videos or exercise programs on TV, even yoga classes. Proper exercise is exercise appropriate to your physical ability and your life stage, so being aware of your physical limitations is also important. I am a proponent of doing something you find pleasurable as your exercise routine, because that's the exercise you'll create time for. For instance, one of the most effective exercises and one that is most appropriate for women going through menopause is walking. Walk with a group of friends. If the weather is bad, then you can go to a shopping mall and use it like an indoor track, walking vigorously around it for a half hour or more. It's very, very important to make sure that you are moving, and that you are moving with ease and pleasure. If you aren't doing anything now, don't start with 45 minutes to an hour. You can start with 15 minutes and gradually increase it every day by five minutes.

I remember when I started my exercise routine, I wanted to do something that did not impact my joints, because I didn't want to be having a knee replacement or a hip replacement when I got to be 65 or 70. I started using the elliptical fitness cross trainer, and when I initially got on that, I could not do five minutes. It was so unbelievable. I thought, "Wow, I am 40 years old and I can't even do five minutes on the elliptical fitness machine." But then I started adding five minutes every day, and now I can do an hour without panting and feeling like I am going to pass out, and I work at the highest intensity level.

Particularly for those of us going through menopause, there have been studies that show there is a direct correlation between weight training and hot flashes and menopausal symptoms. I'm not talking about building muscles, but about balancing your hormones.[38] If you are not a member of a gym, you can do weight training in your own house with cans of food. For about $25, you can buy strength-training bands, which are big rubber bands that you can use in exercising your legs, your arms, and your back.

Another quite effective exercise for mature women is gentle yoga. As we age, we want to keep our flexibility and our balance at optimal levels. One of the most effective ways to do that is to engage in various types of yoga, because yoga teaches us how to breathe better, and it allows us to really stretch those muscles and keep our balance; this promotes better all-around health and stress management.

If you are inclined to use a fitness trainer, just understand that not all certified trainers are created equal. You'll notice many of them are quite younger men and women. Years ago, I bounced from trainer to trainer and couldn't understand why six weeks into the fitness program with someone new, I would hurt something or be in pain of some sort. This puzzled me, because I wanted the guidance of a trainer for a total-body workout. After I did some research, which is typically what I do with all aspects of my life needs, I realized most trainers use a one-size-fits-all fitness routine for their clients. At my age, they were training me as though I was in my mid-20s. What I needed was life-stage-

---

[38] Gretchen Reynolds. The New York Times. Aug. 3, 2016. "Exercise May Ease Hot Flashes, Provided It's Vigorous." https://well.blogs.nytimes.com/2016/08/03/exercise-may-ease-hot-flashes-provided-its-vigorous/?_r=0. Accessed March 2, 2017.

appropriate fitness training, so I searched and found a trainer who was certified in functional fitness. This is an approach that trains men and women like me, "the more mature seniors," to maintain physical health and well-being with appropriate life-stage training. Magic! I no longer get hurt or have the serious aches and pains I used to associate with strength training, because I work out in accordance with my life stage.

Certainly, traditional exercise isn't the only avenue to fitness. Many of us like to dance, right? I had a couple of clients, a husband and wife in their 60s, whom I loved being with because they were so passionate about their retirement. And these folks didn't have a lot of money. I asked them, "What do you guys do to stay so fit and joyful?" because they looked healthy — they were vibrant; they were energetic. They said that they loved to dance and went out dancing a lot. The wife did Zumba, and they got out at least two nights a week and went dancing. They told me that they intended to keep dancing until the day they died. That was an ideal form of exercise for them, because they loved it and it kept them fit and happy.

What is the best kind of exercise for you? It is the kind that you enjoy. Consistent, rigorous exercise to the extent that you can handle it is what's important, because as we mature, exercise is essential to maintain heart health and to minimize the chances that we are going to get one of those ugly diagnoses as we get older. Movement is the key here. Whatever life stage you find yourself in, just keep moving!

Let's not forget that rest and relaxation are forms of gentle exercise for our bodies. I need to be frequently reminded about this by my health coach. As women, we are always doing for everybody else, and we never have time to do for ourselves. Make time! Rest and relaxation are an investment in yourself and in your total well-being, just as important as the other elements required for optimal health. Rest and relaxation help lower stress and boost resiliency. They are very important since, as women go through menopause, our sleep cycles can be disrupted because there are significant hormonal fluctuations that occur in the wee hours of the morning. Also, because women often tend to be more stressed then men, our adrenals are impacted. The bottom line is that we can reduce our stress if we make sure we get plenty of rest and re-laxation and we get quality and sound sleep. Let's talk about relax-ation a bit. While rest means getting the right kind and amount of sleep to rebuild and regenerate your cells, and is needed for opti-mal health, relaxation is where you can get your mind off of your hectic schedule or the stressors in your life while you are awake. This is one of my greatest health challenges, and one that I have yet to master.

Women relax in different ways, and this is all a very personal thing. Relaxation for me is my environment: I live about 1500 feet from the ocean. Relaxation for me is going and looking for shark teeth very casually on the shore, listening to the ocean and all the seabirds. That roar of the ocean, for me, is optimal relaxation. It's the only thing that allows me to turn my mind off of my crazy world of work.

For you, it could be hiking where you get connected with na-ture. It could be playing with your pet or simply walking your dog. It could be listening to your favorite calming music — not wild, crazy music. It could be taking a light nap. It could be going for a manicure and a pedicure or a massage or a facial, or having a very casual dinner with a friend whom you haven't seen in a while. It is anything that allows us to recover at a mental/emotional level, as opposed to a physical level. The degree to which you invest in your rest and relaxation will have a direct correlation to how op-timal your total well-being is going to be, which will serve to de-crease the likelihood of the devastating illnesses that we as women may meet as we move into our more mature golden years.

Let's address the environment really quickly and succinctly. I talked about it in the context of chemicals and such, but the other element that matters is whether your home calms you and brings you joy. This is another area where I had to receive some direct coaching, because I had a tendency to work all over my house. I have stacks of work in my home office, on my bedroom floor, on my dining table. My home was starting to look like a messy workplace, and stealing my peace. It wasn't an atmosphere of relaxation or comfort, but one of disorderliness and chaos — no wonder I could never relax. This impacted my health and my happiness until I cleaned and organized my home and claimed it back as a home and not a workplace.

It seems that when we reach a certain age in our lives, we have a tendency to become hoarders. It may be that we will never get rid of the clothing from our early dating years, or that we have magazines from the last 10 years, or we have a lot of furniture we can't seem to let go of. Rather than looking at piles of clutter, redesign your space as an environment that gives you a sense of peace or serenity. Also, listen to the sounds around you. Do you constantly have TVs blasting so that you can't hear your own thoughts? You probably spend a fair amount of time in your car. Does your car represent more clutter? Look at ways that you create that serenity in your home and in areas where you spend a fair amount of time. Use candles when you are sitting and watching TV; it changes the atmosphere of a room. Clean up your environment by clearing out the closet. I have a philosophy and a practice in my life that I have shared with many of my friends and family: if I go shopping and happen to buy three pairs of shoes and perhaps two shirts, when I get home I have to get rid of two shirts and three pairs of shoes. I will not add to my clothing, because I worry that it's hoarding. Let's face it: 50 percent of what we have in our wardrobes we probably don't even wear. These items may be too small or too big or out of style. If I haven't worn something in three months, pass it along to someone who can use it. That's my method for clearing away my clutter.

If you like to meditate or pray for rejuvenation, where do you do your praying? Where do you do your meditating and your Bible reading? When my spiritual director asked me that, I said, "On my bed." She said that was a no-no; bed is where you sleep. You need a little private place, a spiritual corner in your home that is designated specifically for prayer and meditation. I don't care if it's a closet; the minute you go into that corner, you wind down and you start getting your mind and spirit focused. Have your candle there, and have your Bible or whatever books you prefer to use during the time of rejuvenation. I made my prayer space out of a little corner of my living room, and I feel completely different when I enter this prayer area. I am able to immediately get focused, as opposed to staying in my bed, where I sleep, where I think about things and my mind wanders. So have a very special sacred place for yourself that allows you to have that silence. And communicate that to your family and make sure they all know that when you are in your sacred space, no interruptions at all. Try it; it works!

Emotional Well-Being: Purpose, Passion, and Social Connection

CHAPTER EIGHT

Change, the Challenge

"Someone was hurt before you, wronged before you, hungry before you, frightened before you, beaten before you, humiliated before you, raped before you. ... Yet, someone survived. ... You can do anything you choose to do."
– Maya Angelou

Most significant life transitions occur for women when they're in their 50s. I recently picked up an alarming statistic: Did you know that the average age of widowhood in America is 56?[39] By the time they are 65, most women find themselves alone. Fifty percent of marriages end in divorce, and what we are seeing is a double-digit increase in divorces where the individuals are in their 60s.[40] Children are mov-

---

[39] Illinois Department of financial & Professional Regulation. 2015. "Financial Literacy – Retirement: Widow/Divorce." https://www.idfpr.com/finlit101/Retirement /widow.asp. Accessed Feb. 28, 2017.

[40] Christopher Ingraham. The Washington Post. March 27, 2014. "Divorce is actually on the rise, and it's the baby boomers' fault." https://www.washingtonpost.com/news /wonk/wp/2014/03/27/divorce-is-actually-on-the-rise-and-its-the-baby-boomers- fault/?utm_term=.23d4d77ec5c2. Accessed March 2, 2017.

ing away to pursue their education and careers, and suddenly we are empty-nesters.

All of these are transitions that typically occur when we are going through that physiological transition of menopause. Many women think, *Oh, it's the end of my life. I'm going to be miserable.* But it is one of the most significant life transitions, because it also makes us more aware of our mortality. We have a mindset based on all the media messages that we are getting that our health status is going to change, as if it were a given.

Many times we have an unexpected career transition, because we're being downsized or displaced from what was once a successful career. For years, we have identified ourselves as a teacher or as a professor or a corporate executive, and all of a sudden we are out of work and lose that part of our identity. After a 30-year identification with my working role, what do I identify myself with now? Also at this age, we are becoming more concerned about our financial security.

Suddenly you have all of these factors that lead you to say, Who am I? Where am I supposed to go from here? And what is next for me? What is this next chapter? Almost two-thirds of newly retired boomers (63 percent) in one study said they stressed out over the transition into retirement, citing mixed emotions, the fear of lost purpose or decreased social interaction as factors for their concerns. Yet, the majority said that, a few years in, they grasped a greater control over their lives and were enjoying retirement.[41] Most of us never really think about retirement as a time to reinvent ourselves. We think of it as a time to wind down. The challenge for us as women is to say, "How do I take on this type of

---

[41] Ameriprise Financial. Feb. 3, 2015. "Ameriprise Study: First Wave of Baby Boomers Say Health and Emotional Preparation are Keys to a Successful Retirement." http://newsroom.ameriprise.com/article_display.cfm?article_id=1963. Accessed March 16, 2017.

transition? What can I do to reinvent myself or redefine where I am going to be in the next 10, 20, or 30 years? What will my second act be all about?"

I will use myself as an example to illustrate that it is never too late for that second act. Let's call it your second chapter, your best life yet!

I spent more than 30 years of my life in a caregiving role with aging family members where my purpose was caring for people I loved, and that was a beautiful purpose. I didn't have children. I had aging family members who became like children whom I had to take care of. During those caregiving years, I had an active and intense career in a major corporation, so essentially I had two full-time jobs.

What happened after they passed away and I was alone was quite dramatic and alarming. I realized I didn't know who I was or, even more disheartening, what I had been doing in my life before I started my caregiving responsibilities. I had a very successful executive career that I thought was great. I enjoyed what I did. I worked with great people. I had unbelievable experiences and great opportunities. But all of a sudden it didn't have any purpose, and I lost my passion for my work and for my life. This was quite an emotional and scary time for me because, up until this point, I felt like I had a distinct purpose in life.

I had spent 38 years in corporate America, and all of a sudden I woke up at the age of 55 and I thought, I can't do this any longer. What is next for me? I am still young. I know I want to do something. I just know I can't do what I'm doing. So, at 55, I began a new chapter in my life. I am still writing that new chapter now, and I am very passionate, and I am very purposeful. That's one of the reasons I am writing this book: to send a message out to women that this change in our lives should mark a change in our ability to write a new chapter for our lives — our second act, which is so vital to our total well-being as we journey through the best years of our lives. And rather than being fearful of our mortality, we've got to live life more fully. It should be a message to inspire you, to get you excited about getting out of bed every day and ensuring that you spend time planning for this next phase of your life to be the most beautiful one, with your purpose yet to be discovered. The most innovative business enterprises are yet to be created, the best books are yet to be authored, and the most purposeful journeys are yet to be taken.

When our jobs are taken away, when our supposed physical purposefulness is taken away because of menopause, we can't look at that as diminishing who or what we are. We have to look at these transitions as new beginnings. A new beginning gives us a new ability to have more vitality to start the next phase of our lives, and to nurture those God-given gifts that we have within us that we could not nurture before — because we had children to take care of, we had parents to take care of, we had jobs. We had to make money. We had to put the kids through college and perhaps put our careers on hold to advance our spouse's career.

The fact that our children are off at college or have moved all over the world doesn't leave us empty. It gives us an opportunity to fill that space with a new paradigm and reality. There is energy that comes with that realization, and a new freedom. With those come the need to discover and reconnect with our divine purpose and passion, and that is a very personal experience. I know this from my own life's journey, when I decided I was going to retire from my primary career to reinvent myself and pursue another career. I have more energy and more life at the age of 65 than I ever had when I was in my 30s, because I understand what it is like to work toward something that is so directly in alignment with my personal passion and my values. When you begin to do what you love and what you are truly passionate about, life begins to irresistibly pull you in directions that you never imagined. A personal friend of mine and a certified life coach, Dale Beaman, uses a simple exercise I would like to share here. Take the statement, "When my life is ideal, I am ___," and allow yourself to fill in the blank. Then ask yourself: "What brings me joy? What awakens my passion? What is it that I can soulfully say brings me optimal happiness and fulfillment?"

So fill in that blank, and once you accomplish this task (it is harder than it seems), Dale suggests you make a list of at least 10 things that bring you joy. List as many as you desire, but begin with a minimum of ten. What are the 10 things that would give you a picture of your ideal life? Visualize them, then compare this list of those things that bring you great passion and joy to where you are today. This might lead you to where you can start developing a plan to get you to your ideal life with passion and vitality.

I talked earlier about the client who acquired a horse as her family pet, and she told me, "I feel I am a totally different person when I am with my horse. I am energized and I am happy; I am joyful. And I don't experience that energy and peace without my horse."

So I challenged her with a thought: "Great — if it brings you so much clarity in your passion and your joy, why don't you go get a part-time job taking care of horses?" That suggestion opened the door for her to realize that she could actively integrate her passion into work.

When you are clear about what you want, it will show up in your life, and people will know that you are totally in alignment with your purpose and your passion. You begin to live your authentic life, and it is in this authenticity that you realize what total well-being is all about. If we are not in alignment with our purpose and the passion that drives us to the fulfillment of our purpose, or whatever gives us joy, it can come back to hurt us. I would argue that I created my own cancer 29 years ago, because I didn't understand any of this. I was in a very stressful career and I was working without a clear purpose; I was destroying my immune system. I didn't do anything that brought me joy. I was a workaholic, and that translated into my system as sickness and disease.

In her role as a life coach, Dale often reminds people about what makes the difference between a life lived with intent and a life that is lived thoughtlessly. In one simple but not easy-to-define word, it is passion. Let's talk about the seven keys for living a life aligned with passion.

CHAPTER NINE

Reconnecting With Life

"Love life, engage in it, give it all you've got. Love it with a passion, because life truly does give back, many times over, what you put into it."
– Maya Angelou

Janet Bray and Chris Attwood, in their best-seller "The Passion Test," so simply describe the key principles that are essential to living a life of purpose and passion. As we reflect back on the health-wealth connection, it becomes clear that the degree to which we live a life filled with purpose dictates the balance we find in our emotional and mental well-being, and the happiness we will experience throughout all stages of life, particularly in our very senior years.

It all begins with commitment. Nothing happens unless you are committed to pursuing your life with purpose and passion. As women, we all juggle multiple and often competing responsibilities and feel like we can't do for ourselves. Without commitment, you are undervaluing your worth, and the disconnect can lead to emotional, mental, or physical imbalances and ultimately show up in the financial realm.

After commitment to the pursuit of a life of passion comes clarity. Have you ever met someone who is totally clear on who they are and what they do, and is living life fully? It seems that women who have great clarity about where they are headed and what they want to do project joy and happiness. When you are clear about your purpose and goals — whether it's to lose 10 pounds, save $100 monthly for that special spa vacation, or whatever else you desire — joy and happiness will show up in your life. This is a lifelong process, not a "once-in-a-while" experience.

Commitment and clarity lay the foundation for attention. Focus is critical here, and the things you focus on and attend to consistently and frequently, typically happen. What we focus on grows and then becomes part of our DNA. So if you feel like you need to establish a budget to manage your monthly expenses, the degree to which you focus on that and continue making choices and decisions within the context of the budget determines your financial outcome.

With commitment, clarity, and focus comes the need to be open to whatever is appearing to you at the moment. "Why?", you ask. Because, typically, when you are attentive to what is happening in the present moment, or at this stage of your life, that is when you will seize the opportunity to do something that has been presented to you; it allows us to release our own will and move with God's will, and this is the path to achieving greater happiness. In my journey toward pursuing my passion, had I not been open to closing the door on my career when I was not feeling fulfilled, I would have missed the unbelievable gifts I have been given through learning and growing with women and couples as we developed their life plans.

And finally, it's all about integrity: the greatest challenge we face as women is responding to the demands and the responsibilities we have regarding others. It is equally as important to be true to yourself as it is to be true to others as you are pursuing your passions.

It's fine to talk about "passion," but what's the bottom line? Surprisingly, research shows that there is one: increasing positive emotions could lengthen your life span by up to 10 years.[42]

Negative emotions can lead to serious problems, resulting in physical ailments and thus impacting your health and your wealth.

Numerous studies continue to reveal the damaging results of stress, anger, and hostility on the mind and the body.

On the other hand, studies continue to validate that positive emotions can buffer us from adverse health effects and depression. They enable faster recovery from pain, trauma, and illness. Also, positive emotions have a direct correlation to increases in life spans. A landmark study of 180 elderly Catholic nuns revealed that nuns with more positive emotions lived significantly longer (10 years) than nuns with fewer positive emotions.[43]

Many of us will experience some potentially life-threatening illness at some point in our lives, so the question becomes, "What will I do with that event?" Will you choose to confront it with positive emotions or with doom and gloom? Your answer will either enhance your health and wealth, or it will be significantly detrimental to them.

Are you as close to your family and friends as you would like to be? Do you have enough social connections? Consider your spiritual realm. Are you fulfilled in a spiritual capacity? Do you commit a fair amount of time to nurturing that component of total well-being? Are you in truly fulfilling relationships with people

---

[42] Tom Rath and Donald O. Clifton. "How Full Is Your Bucket?" 6th edition. New York. Gallup Press. 2004.

[43] Pam Belluck. The New York Times. May 7, 2001. "Nuns Offer Clues to Alzheimer's and Aging." http://www.nytimes.com/2001/05/07/us/nuns-offer-clues-to-alzheimer-s-and-aging.html. Accessed March 2, 2017.

who really mean a lot to you, or are you still involved in those toxic relationships that do more damage to you than good?

Do you take regular time out for yourself? Do you give yourself a lot of that "me time," rather than always doing for others? There are ways in which you can do an honest self-assessment; ask yourself these questions, and dig deep into them. This entire book is filled with different ideas and different strategies. This is just a recap of the components that are going to determine what the quality of your lifestyle will be from this point forward.

We talked earlier about what it takes to make changes, so here is a guide. First, what are the one or two goals that you want to establish for yourself? What is it that's easy to change, that you could do within the context of the vision that we talked about earlier in the chapter? What is the realistic vision that you have, and where are those gaps that are keeping you from achieving it?

Our self-assessment moves us up along the change curve. Change occurs only once we've identified that there is a need to change. Self-awareness and taking responsibility — letting go of any anger or frustration, letting go of any of the baggage of the past that is keeping us from reinventing ourselves — allow us to create a beautiful new future. Equally important, as we talked about earlier, is the commitment to the emotional changes, the physical changes, and the financial changes that need to take place.

Make a commitment today to start nurturing your mind, your body, and your spirit. If one of them is out of kilter, it's going to significantly and adversely impact the other components.

How do you do that? For one, ensure that you're getting your annual emotional tune-up. Get yourself a guide or a facilitator, such as a health coach, a life coach, or even a spiritual director. These guides can hold you accountable in the areas that you feel require some attention and development. Give yourself permission to go on retreat; give yourself permission to get away with the girls for the weekend, or do something that you typically would not do. This requires a constant assessment, because many times we may not realize that it's time for that emotional tune-up, and we become numb to those issues that are keeping us from bettering our best, from being the person we are intended to be, and nurturing and awakening that inner spirit within us.

CHAPTER TEN

Reinventing Yourself

"Your power to choose your direction of your life allows you to reinvent yourself, to change your future, and to powerfully influence the rest of creation."
– Stephen Covey

The biggest transitions in life confront most women when they are in their 50s and 60s. Unexpected life events, such as divorce, death of a spouse, loss of a long-term career, taking on responsibilities for grandchildren, as well as responsibilities for an aging parent or friend, can create sudden seismic shifts in our lives. So how do you get through these challenges? Actually, the mindset that got you to the challenges will not be the mindset that gets you through the challenges. We will need to move into a mindset that allows us to reinvent ourselves.

The second act in our lives can be more energizing and exciting, and often just as rewarding and fulfilling, as our first act. The best story is yet to be told, and the best chapters in your life are yet to be written. Let's take a look at some familiar second acts of people who reinvented themselves later in life.

Laura Ingalls Wilder

Wilder's Little House series may be some of the world's most loved children's books, but she was no spring chicken when she sat down to write them. Wilder didn't publish her first novel until she was 65 years old, but she still managed to crank out one of the most popular series of all time.

Grandma Moses

Anna Mary Robertson Moses is one of the biggest names in American folk art, and she didn't even pick up a brush until she was well into her eighth decade. Grandma Moses was originally a big fan of embroidery, but once her arthritis grew too painful for her to hold a needle, she decided to give painting a try in the mid-1930s. She was 76 when she cranked out her first canvas, and she lived another 25 years as a painter — long enough to see the canvases she had sold for $3 apiece fetch prices north of $10,000.

Kathryn Joosten

Kathryn was an unemployed nurse, and at 56 won an Emmy award only after moving in with her son and supporting her family by painting houses and hanging wallpaper. She finally was discovered by an agent who wanted to market her "sassy older woman image." She landed numerous TV roles, beginning with some having only a few lines, and then landed the "old-lady role" in "Desperate Housewives." Kathryn Joosten has won two Emmys for that "Desperate Housewives" role, and it's all because of her uncanny perseverance.

Julia Child

Julia Child changed the way Americans approached food, introducing French cooking to the masses. If you have seen the movie "Julie & Julia," you know that Julia Child did not even learn to cook until she was 40, and she launched her first masterpiece cookbook, "Mastering the Art of French Cooking," when she was nearly 50.

Elizabeth Jolley

Elizabeth Jolley had her first novel published at the age of 56. In one year alone she received 39 rejection letters, but she persevered and finally had 15 novels and four short-story collections published with great success. She has become one of Australia's most acclaimed authors.

Marjory Stoneman Douglas

Marjory Stoneman Douglas was a freelance writer who published her short stories in popular magazines. She wrote her most influential work, "The Everglades: River of Grass," when she was 57 years old. At the age of 78 she started her long fight to protect the Everglades, which she continued until she was well over 100.

So, ladies, if you have not had your big break yet, don't worry; there is still plenty of time for your second act. But don't wait — go for your dreams and never give up. You can realize your dreams if you pursue your passion and find true wealth. You're NEVER too old or too young to create your second act. Mine started at 55 and now, 10 years later, I'm thinking I should invent my third act!

Wealth is not defined simply by your checking account or your investment account values. True wealth is as importantly measured by the following:

1. *Family relationships,* in whatever way you define family, as this is different given culture, environment, etc. Ensure that your family relationships are satisfying to you and serve as a positive life source to you. Are you in any toxic family relationship that drains you? We all know we can pick our friends but we can't pick

our family, but if you have a family relationship that is draining, it's time to separate yourself and increase your net worth. Your God-given worth is being jeopardized by that relationship, so replace it with family relationships that are life-giving.

2. *Social connections* are ever so critical for a vibrant and fulfilling life beyond age 50. When we retire or lose loved ones, we lose important connections and social networks. Many of my widowed clients tell me that, when they were widowed, they no longer fit in with their friends, who were all couples. At a time when friends are so important, a life event like this robs us of key social connections, so we must focus on staying connected in spite of how we might feel. Social networks are critical for retirees, as typically in the world of work our social networks are our colleagues, so when we retire, we lose those connections. I personally experienced this after I retired at the age of 55 and lost those social connections, and felt myself suddenly in a social void. Facebook and other electronic forms of connection do not fill the void. So I sought other connections through women's retreats, church activities, reconnecting with family I had lost touch with, etc. What will you do?

3. *Leisure and fun activities* need to constantly change to ensure they continue to offer relaxation and rejuvenation. This is the key to reducing boredom and keeps us from sinking into depression. As we mature through the various stages of our elder years, we have more time on our hands, and thus can fill time with more leisure activities. True wealth is found in filling leisure time with creative, relaxing, and purposeful activities. It doesn't always mean traveling in a traditional sense, because at some point we are going to wake up and we will no longer be able to travel, or we will have traveled enough, or we will no longer be able to swing that golf club or tennis racket, or we may have some health issue that we have to manage. Regardless of the stage of our lives, leisure and fun need to be a part of our day. So what fun hobbies will you en-

gage in? Book clubs, quilting clubs, volunteering for a nonprofit, tea with the gals, lunch with loved ones, seeing a romantic comedy? Learning a new craft? Writing your story for your loved ones?

4. *Career/work*: The second time around may be your dream. Let's face it, ladies: If you are reading this book and you are 50, 60, or even 70, another career is certainly an option, and not out of the realm of possibility. As we mentioned previously, if you are in your early 60s you could potentially have a 35-year life span remaining. Do you see yourself "retired" for 35 years? Many of my clients who are vibrant and active in their early 80s tell me that they retired too early. We may now have the opportunity to go back to school and get skilled and retooled in an area that fulfills our passion. The second go-around can be one of purpose and passion, and can help us stay connected to a life filled with joy and vitality. This may be the time to pursue a career that improves the lives of others. Recently, as I was helping a client with her retirement plan, I asked what she wanted to do with her retirement, and she was very clear that she wanted to join the Peace Corps and do volunteer work with them. What an amazing second act! She loves to travel and wants to volunteer, so she integrated two interests into one. Another retired couple wanted to work with pet rescues, train therapy dogs, and volunteer with their pets at hospitals and nursing homes. They are joyfully giving back and pursuing their passion. What will you do?

Where Do I Start?

"The secret of getting ahead is getting started. The secret to getting started is breaking your complex overwhelming tasks into small, manageable tasks and then starting on the first one."
– Mark Twain

There are many resources available to women today, but it's important to know the quality of those resources, because we're operating in the information age, and if we Google anything when we try to do research, we'll come up with a wide variety of information, a lot of which will be incorrect. Not all sources are created equal or have a high degree of integrity because the internet is the biggest marketing and sales tool available to us today, and we need to guard against being deceived by that.

In trying to give an example of this for a client, I Googled "Mother Teresa." Now, Mother Teresa, who has now been canonized as St. Teresa of Calcutta, was one of the most amazing figures of charity of our times, unconditionally loving and serving the most unlovable, and I think we all agree that she is truly a saint. Well, when you Google her name, you'll see some of the most awful things about her: about how she's possessed and she's this and she's that. It just goes to show you that we could look up someone really, really good, someone who has helped mankind more than any other individual in our generation, and see some negatives presented online as facts.

That's why I'm providing some valuable resources that will continue to educate and inform you, because I believe good women empowered with good information make the right life choices, whether those choices are in improving their health, improving their finances, or improving their emotional well-being.

Your first and foremost source for information is at www. womans-worth.com and the Woman's Worth® Facebook page. I created this site to be a user-friendly source of information, particularly with relevant information that is informative, inspirational, and allows you to get the facts about women and life planning. Another powerful and empowering website is www.WiserWomen.org, which is the site for the nonprofit foundation, the Women's Institute for a Secure Retirement. It, too, has financial tools, like simple user-friendly calculators that will help you answer all kinds of questions: if you have credit cards you want to pay off, if you have loans that you want to pay off, if you want to refinance or accelerate the payoff of a mortgage, if you want to determine whether a car is affordable for you; there are calculators there to help you figure those answers out.

Additionally, you will find calculators for figuring out what your federal income tax liability might be, and information on optimizing the use of your IRAs. There are estate-planning tools, and saving and investing tools, as well as calculators for budgeting, and for cash-flow analysis. There's a "financial IQ test" that I highly encourage you to take and see what your financial literacy quotient is. If you don't do well, then perhaps you might consider taking a financial literacy program, or this might be the impetus for you to get a financial guide to help you in your journey toward financial independence and, ultimately, total well-being. You'll find wonderful articles and research reports on this site too, especially for women in retirement. For instance, for women going through a divorce or recently widowed, there are unbclicvablc fact sheets and information to help you find out what you are entitled to as you're going through these life transitions.

Another good source of information is the Social Security Administration, www.SSA.gov. This site has a lot of useful materials and great calculators as well. Many women forget that if they were widowed, they can collect Social Security at the age of 60 off of their husband's earnings. Many women don't realize that if they've been a stay-at-home mom, they can collect on their husband's benefit. Or, if they spent 15 or 20 years in a marriage that ended in divorce, they can still claim Social Security off of their ex-husband's working history (the only requirement is that you are unmarried at the time of the Social Security application and you were married for 10 years to your ex). All that information is on the Social Security Administration's website.

The National Family Caregivers Association (www.nfcacares. org) is an unbelievable resource for women. It's got articles and tips, and you can put yourself on a list to get their email blog and receive invaluable information that ensures that you understand all the resources available to you as a caregiver.

The United States Department of Labor, www.dol.gov, has a lot of great retirement information, retirement calculators, and financial fitness calculators. You can request print resources too, which they'll send you at no cost.

I've recently partnered with a firm, Growing Bolder®, which has a powerful website, www.growingbolder.com. Together we have founded the Growing Bolder Financial Institute Powered by Woman's Worth®, in which you will find inspirational, motivational and financial resources and tools. Growing Bolder® is a firm that specializes with "rebranding aging" by providing an online portal of health content oriented toward baby boomers.

Other websites that provide useful information or get you access to resources you may desire include but are not limited to (these are my favorites):

www.dearpharmacist.com

www.easywellnesstoday.com

www.drnorthrup.com

www.dr-gonzalez.com

www.drfuhrman.com

www.growingbolder.com

www.myfitnesspal.com

www.lifemoves.com

Books that address physical health:

"The 24-Hour Pharmacist," by Suzy Cohen, R.Ph.

"Drug Muggers," by Suzy Cohen, R.Ph.

"Eat to Live," by Dr. Joel Fuhrman, M.D.

"Women's Bodies, Women's Wisdom," by Dr. Christiane Northrup

"The Wisdom of Menopause," by Dr. Christiane Northrup

"Breakthrough: Eight Steps to Wellness," by Suzanne Somers

"Knockout: Interviews with Doctors Who Are Curing Cancer," by Suzanne Somers

"Aging Backwards" by Mirand Esmonde-White

"Tox-Sick" By Suzanne Somers

To improve your financial literacy:

"Does This Make My Assets Look Fat?," by Susan L. Hirshman

"Rich Woman: A Book on Investing for Women," by Kim Kiyosaki

"Women & Money," by Suze Orman

For your emotional health:

"The Passion Test," by Janet Bray Attwood and Chris Attwood

"How Full Is Your Bucket?," by Tom Rath and Donald O. Clifton

"Happy for No Reason: 7 Steps to Being Happy from the Inside Out," by Marci Shimoff

"You Can Heal Your Life," by Louise Hay
"Counter Clockwise: Mindful Health and the Power of Possibility"
by Ellen J. Langer

The End of the Story... is the Beginning of the Journey.

I pray that, as you ponder the thoughts and the ideas presented in this book, a seed of action is planted within you to take the first step toward the beginning of the rest of your life — a life characterized by physical, emotional, spiritual, and financial health. Total well-being can be attained, and our second acts can be the best years of our lives, and that promise can be fulfilled in each and every one of us.

Lifestyle Planning Data Requirements

1. Who are the important people in your life?

2. Which areas of your life would you like to receive more of your attention?
    - a. Physical
    - b. Spiritual
    - c. Family/friends
    - d. Hobbies/leisure
    - e. Career
    - f. Financial
    - g. Other

3. Which hobbies, activities, etc. do you enjoy most?

4. What do you want to accomplish during your retirement years?

5. What does financial success mean to you?

If you could design your future retirement, what would it look like? (Where would you live, what would you do, etc? What would be the same; what would be different?)

Once you have envisioned your desired retirement, you will need to gather all information needed to create a life plan which will include but is not limited to the following items. These represent the type and nature of the data required to start building your lifestyle plan:

- Current monthly gross salary
- Estimated annual salary increases
- Projected retirement date
- Projected Social Security benefits (at age 62, 66, or 70)
- Pension income (current and future eligibility)
- Payout dates, options, and amounts for pension benefits
- Pension survivor benefits available
- Total assets earmarked for retirement by type (tax-free, tax-deferred, taxable)
- Contributions to savings and retirement accounts (and % of company match if any)
- Desired minimum asset balance at all times during the various stages of life
- Risk-tolerance assessment
- Current monthly expenses (see worksheet)
- Projected inflation rate
- Type and amount of expenses that will change in retirement (i.e., relocation, mortgage payoff, long-term-care

needs, increase or decrease of anything on the monthly expense worksheet)

- State income tax rate
- Changes in deductions from IRS Form 1040
- Any future adjustments to deductions and year of adjustment (increase or decrease)
- All cash flows (from part-time work, rental income, royalties, inheritance, etc.)
- Life insurance in force by type, duration, and cost
- Cash value of life insurance
- Health of individuals (smoker, nonsmoker, health issues, prescription drugs)
- Family health history
- Health insurance in force and amount of annual out-of-pocket costs
- Disability insurance, if still working
- Annuity contracts inforce and projected income streams
- Long-term-care insurance in force — type and nature of long-term care covered
- Projected desire for utilizing long-term care and funding of long-term care
- Review of legal documents (wills, trusts, powers of attorney, living wills, etc.)
- Desire for gifting for family, charities, foundations
- Tax planning or review of last two tax returns
- Anticipated changes to tax plan
- Special needs of heirs and/or heirs dependents
- Desires for relocation during retirement
- Preferences toward home ownership vs. renting during retirement

Monthly Budget Calculation Worksheet			
Home	**Amount**	**Daily Living**	**Amount**
Mortgage/rent		Groceries	
Home/rental insurance		Personal supplies	
Gas/oil/electric		Clothing	
Water/sewer/trash		Cleaning	
Phone		Education/lessons	
Cable/satellite		Dining/eating out	
Internet		Hair salon	
Furnishings/appliances		Other	
Lawn/garden		**Total Daily Living**	
Maintenance/supplies			
Improvements		**Entertainment**	
Other		Videos/DVDs	
Total Home		Music	
		Rentals	
Transportation		Movies/theater	
Auto loans		Concerts/plays	
Auto insurance		Books	
Registration/license		Sports/hobbies	
Fuel		Outdoor recreation	
Repairs		Vacation/travel	
Other		Other	
Total Transportation		**Total Entertainment**	

Monthly Budget Calculation Worksheet (continued)			
Health	**Amount**	**Savings**	**Amount**
Health insurance		Emergency fund	
Doctor/dentist		Transfer to savings	
Medicine/drugs		Retirement assets	
Health club dues		Other investments	
Life/LTC insurance		Education	
Veterinarian/pet care		Other	
Other		**Total Savings**	
Total Health			
		Charity/Gifts	
Subscriptions		Gifts given	
Newspaper/magazines		Charitable donations	
Dues/memberships		Other	
Other		**Total Charity/Gifts**	
Total Subscriptions			
		Obligations	
Miscellaneous		Student loans	
Bank fees		Other loans	
Postage		Credit cards	
Other		Alimony/child support	
Other		Other	
Total Miscellaneous		**Total Obligations**	

Monthly Budget Calculation Worksheet Total Expenses	
Total Transportation	
Total Home	
Total Transportation	
Total Daily Living	
Total Entertainment	
Total Health	
Total Subscriptions	
Total Miscellaneous	
Total Savings	
Total Charity/Gifts	
Total Obligations	
Total Income Needs	
Total Cash Flow	

a healing meditation
By Louise Hay

I rejoice in each passing year.
My wealth of knowledge grows, and I am in touch
with my wisdom.
I feel the guidance of angels every step of the way.
I know how to live.
I know how to keep myself youthful and healthy.
My body is renewed at every moment.
I am vital, vivacious, healthy, fully alive, and
contributing to my last day.
I am at peace with my age.
I create the kind of relationships I want to have.
I create the prosperity I need. I know how to be
triumphant.
My later years are my Treasure Years, and I become
an Elder of Excellence.
I now contribute to life in every way I can, knowing
I am love, joy, peace, and infinite wisdom now
and forever more.

And so it is!

ABOUT JEANNETTE BAJALIA

Jeannette Bajalia is president of Petros Estate & Retirement Planning, based in Jacksonville, Florida. She is also president and founder of Woman's Worth®, a company that specializes in the unique life-planning needs of women. She was born in Jacksonville and now lives a few footsteps away from the Atlantic Ocean in Ponte Vedra Beach, Florida. After more than 38 years in the corporate world, Jeannette left her executive position with Blue Cross & Blue Shield of Florida in 2007 and launched her second career as a retirement income professional. Since her mission has always been to help people improve the quality of their lives through her work, she views the transition from insurance executive to retirement strategist as a continuation rather than a change of direction.

Jeannette provides guidance on a wide range of financial issues, including lifetime income planning and tax reduction strategies. She holds insurance licenses in Florida, Arkansas, North Carolina, Texas, Wisconsin, Georgia, and Tennessee. Jeannette is the author of "Retirement Done Right," self-published in 2015, and "Planning a Purposeful Life: Secrets of Longevity," which she published in 2017 through Book Publishers Network. Her cut-to-the-chase style of communicating and her keen insight into the financial landscape of retirement challenges and solutions has garnered much attention from the media. She has appeared in The Wall Street Journal and Forbes, and was selected by The Jacksonville Business Journal as one of 20 "Women of Influence" of 2012. In the last few years, she has been interviewed by major TV networks and has appeared on CNBC, Reuters, Yahoo! Finance and MarketWatch.com. She is host of a weekly radio program, Woman's Worth® Radio, which airs on WOKV, 104.5 FM, and has appeared on "First Coast Living" on WTLV. She has been published in periodicals such as Entrepreneur Anchor and Health Source, Investor's Business Daily, Houston Chronicle, and Newsmax. More locally, she has been featured by both The Florida Times Union and Ponte Vedra Recorder, and is a featured speaker for many area women's groups and professional organizations.

Career Path

Jeannette began her corporate career at insurance giant Prudential on the day after she graduated from high school at age 16, and rose to a middle-management position by age 21.

"My parents could not afford for me to go to college," says Jeannette, "So I worked at Prudential in a very demanding position and went to college at night."

Jeannette earned her bachelor's degree in three years while working full time. It took her two years to get her master's degree from the University of North Florida, again while working full time.

When she left the corporate world and approached Petros Financial Services to ask about a position as a financial professional, she did so out of frustration. She had approached five other "financial advisors" seeking advice on what to do with her 401(k) account and the lump-sum payout of her pension plan.

"Those I approached wanted to grab my assets and put them in the stock market without any planning based on my retirement goals or risk tolerance," remembers Jeannette. "And these were high-end advisors who didn't seem to want to understand me or my plans for the future. Under their system, I would have no guarantees that my money would last as long as I might live. I decided I could do a better job myself if only I had the tools. I realized they didn't care about me. ... They only cared about my money."

Her quest led her to Petros. While she says she "only intended to stick her toe in the water" of the industry, just enough to work on her own retirement income strategies, she soon became intrigued with the process.

"It seemed like a natural fit for me to take the training to do this professionally," Jeannette said.

The timing was right, and in a few months Jeannette, now fully "un-retired" and back at work, could build an integrated retirement planning approach and in two short years bought the company. She changed the business model of Petros from a firm that only did insurance sales to being a comprehensive, fully integrated retirement planning firm. She also founded a company, Woman's Worth®, that focuses exclusively on life planning for women. Under her influence, and after purchasing Petros, she expanded the company's services by hiring investment professionals and partnering with tax and legal professionals. Now the company and its strategic partners serve retirees throughout Jacksonville, St. Augustine, Palm Coast, Orlando and all surrounding areas deal with retirement income strategies, estate and tax planning, health care solutions, and insurance solutions.

Family Life

When Jeanette describes her family life, she speaks of herself as a "first-generation American." Her father and mother both immigrated to the United States and she was born here. Hers was a traditional family, deeply religious and rooted firmly in the Middle Eastern culture.

"I saw my mother take care of my grandmother for seven years after her stroke," Jeannette remembers. "There was never a question about it. That's what family means. My father passed away when I was 26 and I ended up taking care of my mother and my aunt until they died; my mother lived to 93 and my aunt to 101."

Jeanette describes her mother and father as hardworking individuals who were the epitome of hospitality, opening their home to anyone in need. She says that they appreciated the opportunity America presented to them. She has fond memories of working behind the cash register at her father's store when she was only 7 years old and getting to know loyal customers.

"They loved the Lord and made sure we knew what was expected of us with regard to upholding the family legacy," says Jeannette. "They would not allow us to abdicate the values we were raised with. They were wonderful examples of 'tough love' and were relentless in teaching us values and morals."

CONTACT

If the information in this book resonated with you and you are looking to take the next step, please, contact us and we'll see if we can get you on the path toward your financial success:

4655 Salisbury Road, Suite 100
Jacksonville, FL 32256
www.womans-worth.com
904.824.5656 | info@womans-worth.com

Made in the USA
Columbia, SC
25 March 2019